TEMPTATION OVERCOMERS

TEMPTATION OVERCOMERS

ELMER L. TOWNS

DESTINY IMAGE® PUBLISHERS, INC.
P.O. Box 310, Shippensburg, PA 17257-0310
"Promoting Inspired Lives."

This book and all other Destiny Image and Destiny Image Fiction books are available at Christian bookstores and distributors worldwide.

For more information on foreign distributors, call 717-532-3040.

Reach us on the Internet: www.destinyimage.com.

ISBN 13 TP: 978-0-7684-6418-4

ISBN 13 eBook: 978-0-7684-6419-1

For Worldwide Distribution.

1 2 3 4 5 6 7 8 / 27 26 25 24 23

CONTENTS

Introduction

OVERCOME TEMPTATION FOR VICTORY

WOULDN'T life be wonderful if there were no temptations in life. That means you could live without facing any possibility of failure. No temptation would be wonderful. But think about it.

If there were no temptations, there would be no success ... no failures. You would not know how close you come to keeping God's standards, or how far you missed His expectations. God would have no basis for rewarding you, or to punish you for failure. Would God have a basis for giving you the benefits of eternal life with Him in Heaven?

But a good God has made it possible for you to enter paradise with Him since Adam and Eve failed when faced with temptation in the garden. Their failure spread to all humans born after them. Only One faced temptation and overcame failure, evil and satan. God's Son, Jesus Christ, was victorious over sin and death and made it possible for all to live forever with God.

Also, if there were no temptations you would lose much of life's motivation. You would miss the challenge of being good, or doing good. You would not know how far short you came from missing the mark (standard) or how well you obeyed God's commandment.

Therefore, temptation can be both good and bad; it can reveal your failure or success.

Look at temptation from a non-moral or non-spiritual point of view. A sign on the street corner says, "No right turn." But you do it anyway ... there was no traffic coming. You did it and did not get a ticket, or a warning from the police. Did you sin, or did you just find a convenient way to get where you were going? Was turning right wrong?

There are many decisions like this in life to tempt us. Are they moral if we obey, or do they make us evil if we disobey? When baking the recipe calls for two cups of flour but you use only one, and if no one notices the difference in the muffins—who cares?! Do you care when the muffins taste great but you did not follow the recipe?

We are all tempted in non-moral ways every day; these deal with man-made rules and sometimes have consequences, and at other times no one cares.

You don't get the car lubricated when the owner's manual requires. You leave your job a few minutes early because your work is done. Because you are late, you walk across a neighbor's lawn when he asked you not to do it. You drive one block the wrong way on a one-way street because there is no traffic.

But on the other hand, there are laws, or codes of conduct, that are put in place by God. Of course there are the Ten Commandments, and beyond them there are other places in Scripture where God draws a line between acceptable and unacceptable behavior.

Think about the Commandment "thou shall not kill" (murder) (Exodus 20:13), the sixth Commandment. But Jesus adds, "ye have heard it said, 'thou shalt not kill ... but I say unto you, whosoever is angry ... without a cause, should be in danger of the judgment'" (Matthew 5:21-22).

But what if they cause us to get angry, and it is their responsibility? Is it still sin when they do something intentional to hurt you? They violate your human dignity. They break God's requirement. Is it sin if you get angry when you suffer the consequences?

GETTING INTO THE TEXT

This series has four sections to help you understand the nature of temptation: where temptation came from; how temptation tries to influence you and others; what are the consequences of giving into temptation; what are some solutions/answers to keep temptation from getting to you.

First, we will examine the temptation of Eve and Adam. We will examine what tactics satan used to get Eve to sin. Then we will look at how satan uses the same tactics to get you to sin; and with that explanation, we will suggest ways for you to be victorious over temptation.

Second, we will look at satan's temptation of Jesus Christ. We will look at satan's strategy in each of his three approaches to tempt the Lord to sin. Then we will suggest principles Jesus used to answer temptation, then apply them to your life.

Next, we will look at the Bible's explanation of temptation and satan's attempts to deceive and get everyone —including you—to sin. In the key verse, 1 Corinthians 10:13, we will see steps a Christian can take to face and overcome temptation.

The last chapter will examine victory-living, and what you can do to live the victorious life.

The title of this book, *Temptation Overcomers*, shows God's purpose to help you overcome temptation, but it involves more. Yes, God wants you to overcome temptation. But even more, God wants you to live above temptation and live victoriously. Yes, God has a triumphant plan for your life.

God wants you to live much better than overcoming temptation. He wants you to claim victory through Jesus Christ. He wants you to exhibit Jesus's power to overcome temptation and live triumphantly. Even greater, God wants the presence of His Son, Jesus Christ, to indwell your life so you live for Him and serve Him. God wants you to live like Paul, who said, "For me to live is Christ" (Philippians 1:21).

But even better than "Christ in you," and even greater than exhibiting your new strength in Christ, God wants you to worship Him for all He is and all He has done for you. Remember, Jesus said, "The Father seeketh worship" (John 4:24).

So, this book is more than overcoming temptation. It is about letting the presence of Jesus Christ live in you and allowing His power to flow through you. This book is about your life bringing glory to the Father, and worshipping Him!

Sincerely yours in Christ,

Elmer Towns

PART ONE

TEMPTATION OVERCOMERS

Chapter 1

THE CONSEQUENCES OF GIVING INTO TEMPTATION

The Story of Adam and Eve

W HAT a wonderful world," Adam said to Eve as they walked across a bubbling brook, entering a lush field of grass.

"I could just sleep here," he pointed to the soft tundra, "but I am not tired."

Eve laughed at her husband. "You never get tired, even with all we have to do," then she laughed shyly—not too loudly; Eve never wanted to criticize her husband.

Each day they enjoyed the warm sun. God had given them the task of tending the garden, the place they lived. It was paradise with all the additions of perfect living. How else could God create an earth? Because He was perfect in His nature and words, perfection was His only way of creating anything.

"What will we eat tonight?" Adam asked. Each night they had gathered a different fruit from a different type of tree. Then Adam spoke what he was thinking.

"Last night we had apples." That was the name of the sparkling red fruit. Each apple hanging from a limb; separated from another. A crisp red protective layer covered the moist juicy white fruit within.

Adam asked, "Did you like the apple more than the grapes we ate the day before?" Red grapes clustered in bunches from a vine. "The grapes were juicier than the apple," Adam reminded his wife.

Eve wanted to remind her husband of what they ate two days ago—bananas. "The fruit was satisfying, but the hard yellow covering was not chewy ... nor satisfying ... I did not eat the peelings, but I love the banana."

"Oh, look at that fruit." Eve pointed to the tree growing in the middle of the garden. Its tall limbs pointed to the sky; its leaves were neither smooth nor rough like the other fruit trees. The singular tree stood alone, not like the other trees growing in clusters, and not attached to other trees. Its roots were not intertwined with the other roots, one tree impregnating another tree. But the time of creation was recent; there had not been time to grow another tree—much less a grove of trees. All the fruit trees of the garden were surrounded with one another; their limbs and leaves grew together. And each grove of trees was surrounded with another tree just like itself; and each had the same kind of fruit.

"But look at the tall singular tree, growing by itself," Eve observed. "It looks so lonely!" Adam joined her to look at the tree.

That one tree growing by itself seemed to tell the other trees, "Don't grow near me ... I don't need your shade ... I don't want to associate with you." Of course trees cannot talk, and this singular tree did not talk, but its lonesome upright position was a message that it was different from all the other trees in the garden.

"What kind of tree is that?" Eve asked.

Adam smiled. He knew the answer, and he knew it was his task to tell Eve about the tree. When God created him, He told Adam,

"You may eat freely of the fruit of every tree in the garden, but you must not eat the fruit of the tree of knowledge of good and evil; if you eat it, you will surely die."

Adam had not told Eve about that tree. They had experimented eating the fruit of all the other trees. And they enjoyed what they ate. But they had not eaten the prohibited fruit; they had not even discussed it yet.

There was a serpent in the tree; a snake had coiled itself around the tree of knowledge of good and evil. To Adam, a serpent was no big deal. He had seen the animal, and one of his early tasks was to give a name to all the animals.

When Adam had seen the thin round snake, as big as his arm, he had named it "serpent." Why? Because that name was who it was.

The serpent was hidden among the green leaves in the tree of knowledge of good and evil; Adam almost did not see the serpent. Looking again at the serpent, whose skin was greenish and brown, the color of the branches and tree trunk, it blended beautifully with the tree of knowledge of good and evil. Adam just smiled. "Good serpent ... good tree ..."

Adam and Eve had talked with one another. They had a vocabulary as large as God wanted them to have, and their thoughts and vocabulary included a definition for every tree, fruit, and bush in the garden. Everything God created had a name and they knew its name instantly.

When Adam and Eve spoke, they knew and recognized the voice of one another and were comfortable with what they heard. Then they talked to God at the end of each day; they recognized His voice calling for them in the garden.

Then both Adam and Eve heard another voice—not their voices, not God's voice—another new voice they had not heard before. The voice was directed at Eve.

"Did God really say you could not eat the fruit of this tree?" The serpent was coiled around some branches of the tree, so she knew the voice was referring to the tree of knowledge of good and evil.

Since the voice was not directed to Adam, he only looked to see who was talking and where the voice was located. He thought about the voice but did not reply. He knew Eve's voice and God's voice, but he did not recognize the voice. Adam thought, *Is this something new I need to learn about in the garden?* He had not heard any other animal talk—just this serpent.

Unknown to Adam and Eve, the fallen angel lucifer had taken possession of the snake. While the serpent was still a snake, and looked like a snake and acted like a snake, it was talking. The former angel—the devil—was speaking through the serpent.

Did Adam think the serpent was the only talking animal in God's creation, or would he find more? Adam did not know what to think.

Lucifer was God's first created being who reflected God's characteristics. He could think, feel, and act. Beyond that, lucifer had the power of self-perception; he knew who he was. He also had the ability of self-direction, the power to navigate and respond according to his internal discretion.

Lucifer was the most beautiful of all the angelic creatures that God created. Because of his self-importance and self-discretion, lucifer decided to exalt himself above all the other created beings. After all, lucifer knew he was the most exquisite and beautiful of all. Also, he knew he was the wisest of all.

Then lucifer decided it was his destiny to advance up to God's presence. When lucifer got that exalted position, he became boastful that he was now equal with God.

Next, the alter-ego of lucifer suggested he was also more beautiful than God and also wiser that God. Lucifer planned to live in that capacity as a co-equal with God. Yes, lucifer's desire was to be co-deity.

Lucifer's brilliance and powerful mind did not warn him that God, who knows all things actual—and potential—also knew everything lucifer was thinking and planning. God looked into the heart and mind of those He created and realized lucifer was planning a rebellion in Heaven. God knew that lucifer was planning to be like Him and to take His place; but lucifer was so limited that he did not realize God's omniscience, that God knew everything, all actual events, as well as all potential events. God knew all thoughts. He even knew what lucifer would think before the evil plan entered his mind.

In an instant, God threw lucifer out of Heaven and away from His presence. Since God had created lucifer as an eternal creature, God could not annihilate him to destroy his existence. God created hell—a burning inferno that would burn for eternity where lucifer would eventually be judged, condemned, and punished. But for now, God allowed lucifer some limited freedom to carry out his evil plan. God allowed lucifer to carry out his evil intentions knowing that with time, He would stop lucifer, condemn him, and forever isolate him in hell.

But for now, lucifer was allowed to indwell the serpent. It was more than indwelling a creation of God's; lucifer would take possession—as in, demonic possession—so that the desire of lucifer could be carried out through the serpent.

Lucifer talked to the woman through the serpent: "Did God really say you should not eat the fruit from any tree in the garden?"

Eve listened to the serpent. She was temporarily transfixed; a serpent was talking to her. Adam heard the serpent speak but did not say anything; the snake was talking to Eve.

Eve had to answer. This was a voice asking a question. Before this she had only heard the voice of her husband, Adam, and God. Now this was mind-stretching; a snake was talking to her.

She answered, "Of course we may eat fruit from any tree in the garden, but God told us not to eat the fruit from this tree in the middle of the garden; we cannot even touch it, because we will die if we do it."

God had told Adam not to eat it; He did not tell Adam anything about touching it. Why did Eve add to God's word something that He did not say? Also, God told them that the day they ate, (immediately) they would die. When Eve answered, she left the time element—day—out of her response to lucifer.

Only later, Eve and the rest of the world would learn that God means exactly what He says. We should obey God's word, not add anything to it.

Lucifer spoke through the serpent: "You won't die." He knew she would not die immediately; she would eventually die a second death in hell where unrepentant sinners are punished. Lucifer told Eve, "God knows the instant you eat, your eyes will be open and you will know good and evil—just as God knows good and evil."

The tree that promised knowledge of good and evil did exactly as God promised. God said don't eat it—but Eve ate the fruit, and she knew good—but in an instant Eve knew what was not good. The fruit would also make Eve know evil—and instantly Eve knew the evil she had committed in disobeying God's command not to eat.

But something happened that made Eve take the first bite. What was compelling? Not her hunger. It was her curiosity; she saw the fruit was beautiful—perhaps more beautiful than any fruit she had seen on any other tree. Also, the fruit looked delicious to her eyes. She had seen the fruit of many trees in the garden, but this was the most beautiful of all in the forest.

But beyond that, Eve wanted the wisdom it promised. Why would Eve want wisdom? She was created perfect, and she knew all she needed to know; and every time she needed to know something new, or more, it was automatically there for her. She knew it immediately.

Because God created Eve perfect, she had a perfect mind. She did not know everything possible and potential; only God knows that. But in her creative innocence, Eve always knew all she needed to know.

Except in this moment of eternity, she forgot God had told them not to eat the fruit of this tree. In that moment of pure, unadulterated freedom, she decided against God's command.

Eve ate.

She gave the fruit to Adam. What was he going to do? What would have happened to humanity if the woman only sinned and not the man? It is a question we don't have the right to ask. It is a question we'll never know.

Adam ate.

Why did Adam eat the fruit that God told him not to eat? No one knows what went on in Adam's mind. Was it curiosity? Was it love for Eve? Was it a lapse of memory? We will never know why Adam ate the fruit. But the freedom God gave in creation was now exercised. He was free to eat, and free to decide. He was free until he ate, then Adam sinned, and all humanity sinned in Adam (see Romans 5:12-14). Adam was no longer free.

She took some of the fruit and ate it, then she gave some to her husband who was with her, and he ate it. (Genesis 3:6 b, NLT)

Both Adam and Eve were created perfect man and woman without sin. They were all that God wanted them to be and they enjoyed daily fellowship with God. But in that eternal moment when they sinned, "they knew they were naked" (Genesis 3:7). Up until they ate the fruit, nakedness was never an issue to them. They walked unashamed before one another, displaying all the glory that God created into their humanity.

But with their sin, a new passion lurked within their hearts. "They knew they were naked" (Genesis 3:7). What would they do? They made clothes.

Men and women have always been inventive, just as Adam and Eve were. Were they created to be appealing and appropriate? Did they make clothing that was both appealing and appropriate to one another? Did they consider whether God would think their clothing was appealing or appropriate? We will never know.

Because God knows all things, God knew what they were thinking and what they did. Because God had created freedom and had given them the freedom of choice, He let them exercise their choice, which they did. So God knew they had sinned long before they realized that God knew. So, what happened next? "They heard the sound of the LORD God walking ... in the presence of the LORD God" (Genesis 3:8)—the sound they had heard on other days when God came to have fellowship with them each day.

Today we cannot image the depth of intimacy and fellowship that Adam and Eve had with their Creator. But those who are saved today have a certain oneness with God as they abide in Jesus Christ and fellowship with God through prayer and meditation. Before the fall, Adam and Eve had this oneness with God, but it was even greater than anything that we who are fallen can understand.

Now they heard the sound again. "They heard the sound of the LORD God walking."

We have no idea what God sounds like when He walks, but Adam and Eve recognized the sound. Even before they could think or react, they heard God calling for them (see Genesis 3:9).

God knew *what* they did, and He also knew *where* they were hiding. And beyond that God knew *what* He was going to do. So why did God ask questions? Not for His knowledge, but for them to realize He knew.

Every time there is a sin, there are consequences; and with consequences, there is responsibility. God asked, "Who told you that you were naked?" (Genesis 3:7).

Notice how the first couple passed the buck, just as people do today when they have been caught telling a lie, or stealing or other forms of trespass.

Adam said, "The woman You gave me ..." (Genesis 3:12).

Eve answered the LORD, "The serpent deceived me" (Genesis 3:13).

The source of Adam and Eve's sin was deeper than the iniquity of the first human couple. The source of sin is in the serpent, i.e., satan. Because satan is the originator of sin and he used the snake to tempt Adam and Eve, God judged the snake. God said he would crawl on his belly (see Genesis 3:19). Up until this time the serpent may have been able to stand upright and do many things that we don't realize today. But then as part of the consequences of his actions, the snake was to crawl on his belly and eat the dust of the ground.

But there was a deeper consequence for satan. There would be eternal conflict between satan and the woman, and that would include her seed, i.e., all of the human race. God said, "I will put enmity between you and the woman, and between your seed and her seed." Thus began the eternal spiritual war of good versus evil, of mankind versus satan, of the followers of God against the followers of satan.

Did you see the word "enmity"? "Enmity" according to the dictionary means hostility, hatred, animosity, or extreme anger. Satan would *hate* people and continually attempt to get them to sin so they would be condemned to eternal punishment—with him.

But there was another aspect of God's pronouncement to the couple. God also said that of Eve's seed, "He shall bruise your [satan's] head and you [satan] shall bruise His heel" (Genesis 3:15).

This is the *proto evangelium*, which means the first giving of the gospel. This is the promise that the woman would have a seed, i.e., children, and ultimately from them would come the One who would bruise the head of satan. Of course, a head wound is a mortal wound. Eventually on Calvary, Jesus would die for the sins of the world to administer a head wound to satan that would eventually cast him into eternal hell. But notice the other half of that promise: satan would bruise the Seed of the woman, who was Jesus Christ. That was the first prediction of the death of Jesus Christ for the sins of all humans. Jesus would actually die a physical death and suffer all the pangs of death. But in victory, Jesus would be raised form the dead to give freedom to those who believed in Him.

EVE'S PUNISHMENT

God laid out two consequences for Eve because of her sin. First, there would be physical pain. God promised in "sorrow ... she would bring forth children" (Genesis 3:16). Therefore, childbearing is one of the most excruciatingly painful experiences that every woman experiences when she gives birth to a child, but it will produce the greatest joy she will have when she brings forth life, her own life in another life, to live beyond her life existence.

But there was a second aspect of Eve's consequences. It had to do with her submissiveness to her husband. God promised, "your desire ... shall be to your husband" (Genesis 3:16).

Adam was not left out. God told him that he would have to work hard, that there would be "thorns, sweat" (Genesis 3:18-19).

TEN LESSONS TO LEARN
ABOUT TEMPTATION

1. Satan is the source of temptation.

Every child of God will be tempted in some area, about some aspect of life. It is usually about their obedience and faith in God. Satan wants every person to sin just as he sinned. And why is that? Satan wants every person to be punished, just as he was punished. That is why he wants every person to sin—sin to death—sin so they end up in hell.

2. Temptation is not good or positive, and it will harm you.

Every time satan brings a delightful temptation, or an enjoyable temptation, or a promise-of-riches temptation, it is never to reward you or strengthen you, or fulfill your life's goals. Satan always uses temptation to harm you.

3. Temptation and its source will appeal to your weakness.

Every person has different strengths and different weaknesses. Satan knows your weaknesses and will attack at your point of weakness, not at your point of sin. And to some he attacks them with the lust of money, i.e., the power of the dollar. To others they are attacked with sexual promises, all to appeal to the lust of the flesh. And still others have weaknesses of ego or pride. Satan knows those weaknesses and will attack a person's weakness.

4. No one is above/beyond temptation in sex,
age, spiritual strength, or any area of life.

Even the youngest Christian who has just been saved will be tempted to fall and/or deny God. And just in the same way, the most spiritual of Christians will be tempted to fall and/or deny God.

5. Temptation comes from without and offers
you various enticements that you may want.

There are all types of enticements to sin, e.g., money, sex, pride, position, whatever. Temptation begins from the outside but aims to get to the core of your being. It will offer you something that you think you may need or desire.

6. When tempting attractions are offered, the
person is not usually aware of its consequences.

Just as Adam and Eve were not aware of the consequences to eating the forbidden fruit, so the average believer is not aware of the consequences when they give in to sin.

7. Temptation usually appears in the form of
physical enticement, emotional gratification,
or egotistical enhancements.

Temptation approaches each person differently according to their weaknesses or desires. Therefore, temptation for one person may not at all appeal to another. While God knows all things, satan knows many things, and he knows the weaknesses of each person and appeals to their weakness.

8. The consequences of giving in to temptation are absolute.

Sometimes the consequences are immediate and devastating; at other times it takes time for consequences to happen. Consequences can be physical, financial, emotional, family, or business related. At other times consequences may not appear for a while, and sometimes consequences may be administered in eternity when the person is cast into hell. Or the Christian who gives in to temptation in this life is not given rewards or crowns when they appear before the Judgment Seat of Jesus Christ.

9. God knows you are human and offers a solution of forgiveness.

Long before you were ever born, long before the creation of Adam and Eve, God, who is eternal, looked over the annals of time to see the struggles of every believer against sin. Whereas the cross of Jesus Christ happened at a specific time, at a specific place in Jerusalem, through a specific instrument of punishment, i.e., the cross, God applies the blood sacrifice of His Son for your sins to forgive you according to His mercy and grace. Because of God's faithfulness, He will forgive sins; and because of God's grace, He will help you through your temptation.

10. It is your responsibility to confess your sin, accept forgiveness, and live in a new relationship to God and serve Him.

Jesus died for your sins. When it comes to forgiveness, God saw the blood of His Son and forgave your sins based on the merits of the perfection of Jesus who died for your sins. Now it is your responsibility to confess your sins (see 1 John 1:9) and accept forgiveness (see Ephesians 1:7) and live in a new relationship to God (see Galatians 2:20) and serve Him (see John 15:7).

Chapter 2

LET JESUS SHOW YOU HOW TO FACE TEMPTATION

Jesus's Answer Was Quoting Scripture

MATTHEW 4:1-11

DARK clouds scurried across the winter sky above the mountains. The raw winter wind whipping down off the Sea of Galilee chilled His flesh. Jesus was tiring. He had traversed one hill after another toward this valley in the Judean mountains, uninhabited peaks barren of plant and animal life except for a few resourceful predators and the scavengers waiting for them to die of starvation.

The Spirit of God had led Jesus to this desolate place for a reason, but He was not alone; an evil presence shadowed the man from Nazareth.

Jesus crossed the Wadi Qelt and began to climb the rocks, then stumbled into a remote mountain pass flanked on either side by formidable cliffs. Because of its rugged ascent through rocks and narrow ravines, a casual observer would likely dismiss this path as a dead end. However, the Spirit kept leading Jesus upward until He reached a narrow ledge overlooking a deep canyon.

Nearby, a spring of water trickled through the rocks and Jesus drank from it. Although He was fasting, Jesus allowed Himself life-sustaining water while abstaining from solid food. He followed the spring to a cave that would protect Him from the elements.

A red serpent hissed and slithered out from under a rock and slid a short distance down the path. The serpent coiled in a murky, wet crevice and watched Jesus. Across the ravine, two ravenous wolves stood in a darkened cave, also watching Jesus, who had invaded their canyon. Jesus ignored them. Soon, He knew, a far more dangerous predator would stalk Him to this place.

Jesus lay exhausted on the cave floor but could not sleep. He had committed Himself not to eat any food for forty days, but there was an emptiness deep inside that bread and food could not fill. He longed for the presence of the One without whom He was incomplete. Jesus was hungry for God. "Father!" He cried out, "I seek Your face. I will do Your good and perfect will."

The days passed; the weather turned mean. A storm rumbled through the valley, the dark underbellies of the clouds unleashing their frigid contents upon the mountain with stinging fury for several days. Jesus shivered in the cave, out of the wind and rain. His bones creaked; His muscles ached. He pulled His cloak tightly about Him.

As Jesus approached the end of His fast, He found that He was lonely. He had not heard the friendly sound of another human voice for forty days. Life is good, Jesus reminded Himself, and made to be shared. Jesus smiled as He remembered His family . . . meals . . . sitting with friends, drinking in the beauty of the Galilean hills.

A snowflake softly lit on the back of His folded hands. Then another. And another. Lifting them to His eye, Jesus tried to see their unique patterns, but the overcast sky and the darkened cave kept them hidden in darkness. Though rare, snow did fall sometimes high in the Judean mountains. Jesus prayed again before dozing peacefully with the white flecks drifting gently in the ravine.

The next morning Jesus awakened to a sound—a sound out of place—like the squeak of a chariot wheel. Then He recognized the chirping of a bird. A bird was singing. Morning washed away the night, and Jesus saw shadows across the ravine. The sun peered through the canyon walls down into the ravine, like sunshine through a crack in a closed door. "The sun," Jesus said aloud, smiling as a golden sliver warmed His tired body. "God is good." He thanked the Father for the dawning of a new day. He was ready to do battle.

His adversary, satan, had been waiting and watching, having followed Jesus to this desolate location. And now that Jesus was in a physically weakened condition, the devil would call upon every device, every wile, every work of evil to bring down the Son of God. Satan knew something of the power that lay within Jesus's grasp, and he wanted that power. He wanted Jesus to dangle helplessly like a puppet at the end of his string.

The devil came to Jesus in the small clearing. "If you are the Son of God," he challenged Jesus, "command these stones to become loaves of bread. You must be hungry. You have the power to change the stones into bread."

Memory can be a terrible master, for it reminds us of better days and tempts us to return to a past that is prohibited to us, and Jesus now remembered the bread His mother baked in the community oven in Nazareth. The stones before Him were brown like small round loaves of bread. The aroma of fresh bread drifted through Jesus's memory. He could do it. He could turn the stones to bread ... bread just like his mother baked ... with butter, if he desired. But the Father had sent Him to serve mankind, not Himself.

"No," Jesus said to the tempter. "It is written, 'Man shall not live by bread alone, but by every word that proceeds from the mouth of God.'"

Jesus knew the strength of resolution—and it nourished His soul—it came from the words of God.

Satan, still confident of victory, changed tactics. The two enemies were then transported to the pinnacle of the Temple in Jerusalem, where they could look down on Jerusalem—and Jerusalem could see them. There they stood atop the religious world. Satan challenged Jesus, "Since you are the Son of God, throw Yourself down!"

Satan paused for dramatic effect. "Surely You are not afraid. Is it not also written, 'God will command His angels to protect You, and they will lift You up in their hands, so that You will not so much as strike Your foot against a stone'?" The devil, too, could quote Scripture, though twisted for his own purposes.

Jesus neither moved nor responded.

"The people want miracles," the devil urged. "Throw Yourself off the pinnacle. The angels will save You ... people will believe in You."

Jesus could indeed do miracles, but He would not do one for satan. He would do only the will of His Father, and this was not His will. Jesus answered the devil, saying, "It is also written: 'Do not tempt the Lord your God.'"

Then they were whisked to the peak of a great mountain. From there, they looked out on the beauty, the majesty, the glory of all the kingdoms of the world. They could see beyond the hunger; they could also see beyond the curtains of time. "Look at the people," the devil said to Jesus. "Look at the thousands ... millions ... multitudes."

In one transcending moment, Jesus saw the nations of the earth; He could see the future pages of history unfolding before Him. People, each a living soul, made in the image of God. People that God loved. People ... the reason why God created the universe and the earth. *They are the reason why I have come*, He thought.

"I am the god of this world," satan boasted, "and these are my people." Jesus did not deny this; He was familiar with the devil's claim. Satan reigned on Earth, and he enslaved its people. Jesus's heart ached for the millions held captive by sin.

"If you bow down to me," the devil sounded so convincing, "if you bow down to me," he propositioned, "I will give all these people to you."

No mortal man will ever know how deeply Jesus was tempted to strike this bargain with the devil, because mortal men cannot fathom the depths of God's love. They will never love the people of the world as Jesus loved them at that moment.

"The world will be Yours! Only kneel down," the devil coerced. "Worship me. Now!"

"Away with you, satan!" Jesus answered. "It is written, 'You shall worship the Lord your God, and you shall serve Him only.'" Then the devil left Him, and behold, angels came and ministered to Him (see Matthew 4:10-11).

Satan tempts Jesus in each of the three areas in which people are tempted today. Although Jesus was God and could not by nature sin (see James 1:13), the temptations were nevertheless very real. Jesus overcame the temptation of satan by relying on God's Word, rather than upon Himself. Three times Jesus answered satan, "it is written" (Matthew 4:4, 7, 10). In doing so, Jesus gave His disciples a pattern to follow in their struggles with temptation.

HOW SATAN TEMPTED JESUS

1 John 2:15-17	Matthew 4:1-11
Lust of the flesh	Stones to bread
Lust of the eyes	Glory of kingdoms
Pride of life	Prove deity with a miracle

Jesus's victory over satan in the wilderness was not the last time the two would engage in spiritual conflict. Later, satan would use a natural storm to tempt the disciples to not trust God. Even one of Jesus's closest disciples attempted to destroy or sidetrack Jesus from His Messianic work. Ultimately, the cross itself was Jesus's most intense battle with satan. But at the beginning of His ministry, in the wilderness, He overcame satan and his attack at its most basic level. In at least one sense, Jesus's victory over satan in the wilderness marked the beginning of the end for that fallen angel.

TEN LESSONS ABOUT VICTORY LEARNED FROM JESUS

1. Be strong! Spend time with the Father in fellowship and prayer, fasting as you worship and obey Him.

2. Be watchful, but don't live in fear of any temptation or attack from the enemy, but focus on worshipping the Father and walking in obedience with His Son, Jesus Christ.

3. Be prepared to stand against temptation. Face each new day and each temptation knowing that you will be targeted with temptation because you live in fellowship with the Father. Yet in that conformation, know that Christ will give you the victory.

4. Be always diligent. You will not be exempted from temptation in your Christian walk with God the Father, just as Jesus—who never sinned (see 2 Corinthians 5:21)—was not exempted from temptation. But realize you can be victorious over temptation, just as Jesus was successful over temptation.

5. Be ready with your weapon of defense. A sure way to overcome temptation is knowing and quoting the Scripture, just as Jesus used Scripture when tempted.

6. Be wise about temptation and its source. There are many forms of temptation, and they come with various enticements and will appeal to various areas of your life, just as Jesus was faced with various temptations from satan in various areas of His life.

7. Be ready always to refuse temptation in one area of life and get victory over that temptation. It does not mean you have final victory; other temptations will come against you in other areas of life, at other times in your life.

8. Be vigilant. If you overcome temptation and it leaves you, remember that just as satan left Jesus but returned in another way, so too satan and temptation will come again against you.

9. Be confident; Jesus is your example for overcoming temptation so you can overcome temptation just as He overcame temptation.

10. Be thankful for every victory God has given you over temptation in the past. Rejoice in what the Lord has done for you. But remember, just as satan left Jesus to return on another occasion, so too satan will be back to tempt you in the future. It may be a

different type of temptation in another area of your life, but he will return. Therefore, be ready always, and look to Jesus who is your example of victory and your strength in battle.

Chapter 3

PROTECTION AGAINST TEMPTATION

PRINCIPLES THAT GIVE VICTORY

*You will not be tempted to sin with any
greater enticement than any other believers
have faced, but you can be victorious over
your temptation. Remember, God is faithful
and will not let you be tempted beyond your
ability to resist it. He will always make a
way to endure it without yielding to it.*

1 Corinthians 10:13, ELT

WHEN a loving mother knows there is going to be rain and storms, she wraps her children in a raincoat before sending them off to school. That is the ultimate expression of her love because it protects her children. Love is why God has provided protection for His children against temptation.

When you buy a house, you know it is going to rain, and worse than that, it may snow and there will be sleet. So make sure there is a roof covering of asphalt, tin, or whatever to keep out rain and snow. And when you know a snowstorm is coming, make sure the home is insulated against freezing rain. That is the expression of a wise homeowner. In the same way, a wise Christian will take advantage of all the protection available against temptation.

When a person opens a store, or begins selling to the public, or launches a business, they build in safeguards to protect their money, their reputation, their assets as well as the future. Those are the ingredients of a wise businessperson.

THINGS TO KNOW
ABOUT TEMPTATION

1. Temptation will surely come.

Paul wrote to the Corinthians to alert them that they would be tempted to sin with enticement from satan. In the same way, you will face temptation. Just like all other believers have faced temptation. But Paul went on to promise they could be victorious over their temptation, and he offered them the glorious prospect of defeating temptation, saying, "But thank God He gives us victory over sin and death through our Lord Jesus Christ" (1 Corinthians 15:57, NLT).

2. Your temptation does not come from God.

Sometimes Christians who have dedicated their life to God, and attempt to live for God, wrongly blame God for any temptation that tries to ensnare them. James writes, "Let no one say when he is tempted, 'I am tempted of God.' God cannot be tempted by evil, nor does He Himself tempt anyone" (James 1:13). No, your temptation does not come from God.

3. Your temptation comes from your adversary—satan.

While you will never see satan, nor actually hear his voice, he will use situations, events, people, and your fleshly desires to trip you up into sin. Remember, satan is wise, smart, and crafty; he knows sin, and he knows your weaknesses. Remember, "your adversary the devil walks about like a roaring lion seeking whom he may devour" (1 Peter 5:8).

4. Temptation gets to you through your sinful nature.

When God saved you, He forgave all the sins against you. Because of His mercy and grace, He not only cleanses your record in Heaven, He pronounces that you are His child and you have the righteousness of Jesus Christ (see 2 Corinthians 5:21). That great awareness should give you strength to overcome any temptation. But you still have a sinful nature. Even when you try to walk in fellowship with God and keep your eyes on Jesus, be careful of your deceitful old nature that will attempt to draw you away from fellowship with God. "But each one is tempted when he is drawn away by his own desires and enticed" (James 1:14).

5. Temptation is designed to destroy you.

If all satan wanted to do was for you to follow Him and please Him, that might be an excuse to some to give in to temptation. However, satan wants more than your allegiance; he wants more than your soul; he wants you destroyed in hell with him. Why? Because God has already planned to throw satan in hell at the end of time where he will suffer for all eternity. Satan wants you to be there with him and will drag you into temptation to destroy you. "Temptation ... when desires have conceived it give birth to sin, and when sin is fully grown, it brings death" (James 1:14-15).

6. No one is exempt from temptation, even those who walk close to Jesus Christ.

When you think in terms of the disciples walking with Jesus on a daily basis, they not only saw Jesus, they heard Him and enjoyed His presence. But even then, two disciples gave in to temptation. The first was Peter, who gave in to temptation to deny Jesus Christ—three times. After he sinned, Peter went out and wept bitterly. Was it because he had sinned? Because he lied? Or because he broke his intimate relationship with Jesus Christ? The other disciple who was tempted was Judas Iscariot. He was the trusted one who carried the money bag for Jesus and the other disciples. Just as temptation successfully got into the heart of Peter, it also destroyed the life of Judas Iscariot. "The devil had already put into the heart of Judas Iscariot ... to betray Him" (John 13:2).

WHERE WILL SATAN ATTACK?

Do not love the world or the things in the world. If anyone loves the world, the love of the Father is not in him. For all that is in the world—the lust of the flesh, the lust of the eyes, and the pride of life—is not of the Father but is of the world. (1 John 2:15-16)

Temptation gets to us through our human existence, i.e., our physical, mental, emotional, or spiritual existence. Temptation uses the three doorways to reach us, or entice us. These doorways are the lust of the flesh, the lust of the eyes, and the pride of life.

What does this mean? Usually lust has a sinister meaning, identifying the lower or evil things you desire but should not have. However the word "lust" sometimes is translated as just "desire" and/or the things you want or the things you need.

Lust usually involves things that will please or satisfy the needs or desires of the physical body. There are good lusts, such as you need water, food, and of course you need air to breathe.

But when we talk about lust, it is not just the food you desire; it is when you fulfill that desire in the wrong way, doing it wrongly for the wrong reason. If you lie to get money so you can get food, lust has used a natural desire, i.e., hunger, but fulfilled it by sinful means, i.e., telling a lie. When you cheat or steal money that is entrusted to you —because you are a cashier or salesperson or a company representative—then lust has gotten the best of you.

Lust usually begins by convincing you that you need an object, then enhances your desire for that object, and finally motivates your passion to do anything to get it.

The lust of the eyes. This usually involves things that we see that attract our attention. This can be a desire for money, possessions, clothes, luxuries, or even the tools we need to live. Lust is wanting any object or ability more than anything else, and we are willing to pay any price to get it, even breaking the law, violating our conscience, breaking the Ten Commandments, or disobeying God; then that desire becomes lust, and fulfilling that lust becomes sin. When the Bible speaks about the lust of the eyes, it is focusing on the eye gate that brings the outside world into our thinking. Please understand that seeing things is not wrong; sin is seeing and desiring and planning to get or use things that are wrong.

You will see many things in life that you should not see, you will see things that are contrary to God's plan, and you will see things that are definitely sin. When you see a person steal something, you have not sinned in merely seeing it. However, when you see that person get away with the things they steal, and that entices you also to steal, then what you have seen with your eyes has become lust and leads to sin.

The pride of life again deals with a very difficult area of life. In one sense a person should be proud of the family that gave them birth, defend his/her family, and work hard to enhance the reputation of the family. In the same sense a person can be proud of the job they have, and they can also be proud of the accomplishments when they do their best for the job. This could be simply ego strength, because they have a strong self-direction, self-identification, and self-purpose in life. They have come to know themselves, to know their strengths, their purpose in life, and they can make a positive contribution to the things in life.

But pride involves ego enhancement, when a person wants credit for something they do not deserve, when they want attention for accomplishments they have not attained, or when they desire a position they should not have because of Christian standards or their Christian testimony. Pride is simply claiming to be what you are not.

WHAT TO DO IF YOU GIVE IN TO TEMPTATION

As a Christian you will face temptation from many different sources, in many different attractions, appealing to many different needs or desires in your life. Temptation comes to all people, no matter how spiritual or how strong you are in your faith. Facing temptation is part of living, and by it we face the world ... the flesh ... and the devil. These three bastions of evil are determined to infiltrate every life—your life—with the view of destroying every life—your life—and plugging all souls into hell—your soul.

Your primary task in life is not spending your time and energy thinking how you can avoid evil; your task is to please God. Yes, your goal is to not sin, but to live as perfectly as possible. Remember, the Scriptures say, "these things I write to you, so that you may not sin" (1 John 2:1).

The only person who is perfect is Jesus; you are not. You were born in sin (see Psalm 51) and you sin continually (see 1 John 1:8, 10).

Remember, Jesus was tempted, yet He did not give in, but you might. Everyone has been tempted, "each one is tempted" (James 1:14).

What does that mean? No one has a perfect track record when it comes to sin. "If we say we have not sinned, we deceive ourselves" (1 John 1:8). So there is no perfect Christian among us; we all are sinners, we all must stand strong against sin, and we must seek victory in Jesus Christ.

Years ago, when I was attending Dallas Theological Seminary, I had a weekend pastorate in west Dallas. One day I was building an extra room in the church sanctuary when some little boys came to watch me as I was constructing a wall. I stopped to share the plan of salvation with the boys and I mentioned to them that each of them was a sinner. One little boy said, "I never sin." I had never had anyone tell me that, so I inquired, "Have you ever cussed or used God's name in vain?"

"No."

"Have you ever stolen anything, i.e., even a penny?"

"No."

"Have you ever told a lie ... even a small lie?"

"No."

Then one of the other boys gave his opinion: "He is sinning now—because I have heard him lie many times."

Whenever you sin, remember you have a Savior who has a solution to your sin. If we were left to ourselves, we could not gain life with God beyond death. But God gave us a Savior, Jesus, who understands us and died for our sins. So, what should you do with your sins? "You have a High Priest who cannot sympathize with our weaknesses, He was tempted in all points but did not sin. Come boldly to His throne of grace, to obtain mercy and find grace" (Hebrews 4:15-16, ELT).

So when you come to God, confess your sins. And what does the word "confess" mean? From the bottom of your heart, honestly recognize you are a sinner, and confess your need of salvation. "If we confess our sins, He is faithful and just to forgive ... and cleanse" (1 John 1:9). When we confess our sins, God forgives us our sins, and we can walk in fellowship with Him again.

Then repent and determine not to do it again. It is one thing to be forgiven of sins, but do we run back to God continually asking for continual forgiveness when there is no intent in our hearts to turn from our sins and follow God's plan for our life?

The word "repent" means to acknowledge in your mind that you have done wrong and admit outwardly to God in confession that you are a sinner. Then commit yourself to walk in fellowship with God, obey God, and seek His presence. "Create in me a clean heart, O God, and renew a steadfast spirit within me" (Psalm 51:10).

When you confess your sins, God forgives and He remembers them no more. Sometimes the problem is our human memory. We remember our mistakes and are plagued with a guilty conscience. Sometimes we remember our mistakes and do not have remorse. So we continually go back to beg God for forgiveness without walking in His forgiveness. And even some remember their sins and, rather than turn from them, they go back to it to try it once again.

TEN THINGS GOD PROVIDES TO RESIST TEMPTATION

1. Prepare with prayer.

You should be aware that temptation is everywhere, and if you have not been tempted today, eventually you will be tempted—probably where you did not expect it. When it is daylight, remember night is always coming. When it is summer, plan on winter. So, when you are walking with God, remember that temptation will come. It is inevitable. Pray daily the Lord's Prayer, especially the petitions "Lead me not into temptation, but deliver me from the evil one" (Matthew 6:11, ELT). This verse can be translated to say, "Lord, don't lead me into temptation where I will be tempted above my ability to resist, but when temptation eventually comes, give me a way of escape so I can be victorious."

2. Begin by yielding to God.

Every day you need to give the control of your life to God. Just as you pray the Lord's Prayer every day to not be led into temptation, you should also pray, "Thy will be done." Make sure you include, "Thy will be done in my life ... this day ... in every way ... for all purposes." And how can you do this? James tells us, "Submit yourselves therefore to God. Resist the devil and he will flee from you" (James 4:7). This verse has the two-way secret of victory: first, yield to God; and second, resist satan.

3. Keep on resisting.

Yes, you can face temptation and be victorious, but remember, satan will come back time and again. But make up your mind before the day begins that you will not sin. "Be sober, be vigilant; because your advisory the devil walks about like a roaring lion seeking whom he may devour" (1 Peter 5:8).

4. Trust God for victory.

Yes, read the Scriptures and pray for victory. Then remain resolute against sin. But do not trust in yourself. Put your trust in God, for He is the strong One who can give you victory over sin. "The Lord knows how to rescue the godly" (2 Peter 2:9).

5. Claim Jesus's intercession for you.

When you begin to pray the Lord's Prayer, "Our Father..." (Matthew 6:9), that personal pronoun "our" means that prayer was given to you by Jesus. So He is inviting you to approach the heavenly Father with Him in prayer. So you pray to God the Father with Jesus Christ, asking for victory over the evil one. But also remember, more than Jesus praying with you, He is interceding for you in Heaven. "For we ... have a High Priest ... let us come boldly to the throne of grace, that we may obtain mercy and find grace to help in time of need" (Hebrews 4:15-16).

6. Follow Jesus's example of victory over satan.

Jesus, the Son of God, was tempted to sin in three ways and He did not sin. Each time, Jesus quoted the Word of God when resisting satan. You should do the same. Read the Word of God, memorize it, and quote it when tempted. Quote it to yourself, and sometimes speak it outwardly. This is the tool Jesus used in victory over sin. "For in that He Himself ... being tempted, He is able to aid those who are tempted" (Hebrews 2:18).

7. Put on the whole armor of God.

Remember, you fight satan, who is more powerful than any human; you also fight sin, which is devious and will destroy you. And then you live in a world system that is continually enticing you to enjoy its pleasures, and ultimately to suffer the consequences of its destruction. So what can you do? "Put on the whole armor of God that you may be able to stand against the wiles of the devil" (Ephesians 6:11).

8. Memorize and meditate on Scripture.

God's Word is more than a record of God's people in Bible times, and it is more than a narrative of the life, death, and resurrection of Jesus Christ. The Bible is the Word of God (see Hebrews 4:12) that contains God's plan and God's life. The Bible is alive with the life of God. When you hide God's Word in your heart, you are putting God in the center of your thinking and being. When you memorize and meditate on God's Word, you are asking God to control your life and thinking. "I have hidden Your Word in my heart that I might not sin against You" (Psalm 119:11).

9. Always plan to do right.

When you leave home with plans to go to the store for something, you don't get sidetracked to pursue a hobby, or visit friends, or to do any of those other things that keep you from your plans. Rather, when you plan to go to the store, it becomes the primary control of your thinking. In the same way, always plan to do the right thing in the right way at the right time for the right purpose. Always plan to do right so you will be right. Paul tells us, "Be not overcome by evil, but overcome evil with good" (Romans 12:21).

10. Walk in faith and fellowship with God.

Just as you were sincere when you asked God to forgive your sins, now walk sincerely in faith-fellowship with God. This is called *faith-walking*.

Chapter 4

AFTER OVERCOMING TEMPTATION

Victory-Living

IT is wonderful to think about overcoming temptation. But what about the next time? What about the next temptation you face? Will you rely on the same steps that first gave you victory over temptation?

Rather than thinking about minimizing temptation, let's think about victory-living. Let's talk about what you must do to live for God after you overcome temptation. This chapter is about the principles you must follow to enjoy victory-living.

Just as salvation involves two steps, i.e., first repent, then believe, so too victory-living involves two steps. First you learn what you must not do to live above sin. Then, at the same time—you begin both actions at the same time—you learn positive things to obey God, to please Him, and bring glory to Him.

LEARN WHAT NOT TO DO

1. You must not disobey God's commands.

The Westminster Confession of Faith asks the question "What is sin?" The first part of the answer gives a clue: "Sin is any lack of conformity or transgression against the law of God" (ELT). Anything that does not conform to God's Word is sin.

When a mother says to her son, "Go to the store and get bread," and she finds him playing baseball on the corner, what should be her reaction? She cannot be happy. He has disobeyed his mother by not obeying her (see Ephesians 6:1). If he continues, a serious flaw may develop in his character.

There are certain commandments that are easy to obey, meaning there is no question about what the Christian should do. First, reading your Bible, praying, and watching for His Second Coming. Then you are to tithe (see Malachi 3:10), attend church (see Hebrews 10:25), confess your sins (see 1 John 1:9), and love other Christians (see John 13:34).

When a father asks his 12-year-old boy to wash the car and he forgets, it is not as bad as his twin brother throwing mud at the car. The father is displeased with both sons, and he deals with each offense differently. But he can't overlook the one who didn't wash the car. The Scriptures teach, "Therefore to him that knoweth to do good, and doeth it not, to him it is sin" (James 4:17, KJV).

The Ten Commandments are negative warnings: "thou shalt not...." You sin when you go against God's commandments. God says it is wrong to kill, lie, steal, commit adultery, and have idols in your life (see Exodus 20:3-17).

The commands of God are not grievous; we obey Him because we love Him. Some have mistakenly thought, *All pleasures in life are gone now that I am a Christian*. God is not a mean Father who locks His children in a closet to keep them safe. But like a wise father, God knows some things will harm His children. What parents would allow their children to play near a busy highway or in a field with snakes?

For some things God says no. Don't see how close you can get to the edge. Understand why God said no. When you understand God's purpose, obey with enthusiasm.

2. You must follow your conscience.

Your conscience is a moral regulator that flashes information to the brain. It tells you what it thinks is right and wrong. Like the thermostat in a house when things get chilly, it starts the furnace. When your conscience tells you something is wrong, don't go against it. At birth the conscience reflects the image of God in you. The original conscience tells you it is wrong to murder, steal, and lie. God brands these moral issues in your heart.

My father was an alcoholic. I saw the misery he caused my mother. We children had to do without because he drank so heavily. I don't know if alcoholism is in-born or if a person becomes an alcoholic by taking the first drink. But I've always had a fear of liquor of any kind. I did not want to be a drunk like my father.

I once refused communion because real wine was served. I will not eat meat cooked in liquor in any form, even though the alcohol is burned off. I feel that if I got one taste, I might become an alcoholic. Some may think I am narrow, but I will not go against my conscience. "Therefore to him that knoweth to do good, and doeth it not, to him it is sin" (James 4:17, KJV).

While I feel it is wrong to ignore your conscience, some say, "Let your conscience be your guide." This could be bad advice. Your conscience cannot always be trusted. Your conscience can be "educated" to not feel the wrongness of some situations. The conscience can be "seared": "having their own conscience seared with a hot iron" (1 Timothy 4:2). This pictures a hot poker burning a scab on the skin. The conscience is seared when one continually goes against its instructions. Then the conscience will no longer tell you when you violate it, i.e., do wrong.

Note the following guidelines for your conscience. First, everything your conscience tells you to do may not be right. Some people think it is allowable to steal or lie under certain conditions.

Second, your conscience won't tell you everything that is wrong. The conscience depends upon the training it has received. Some people commit adultery not realizing what God has said about sexual purity.

Follow your conscience to a certain extent. But pray daily that God would enlighten it. But don't let your conscience be the final deciding factor in what you do for God.

3. Do not harbor impure thoughts.

We live in a "girl watchers" age. Men enjoy surfing the internet for porn, or walking the beaches to look at the bodies of girls in their bikinis.

Sinful thoughts involve more than physical touch. It is a sin to look and lust. Jesus said, "Whosoever looketh on a woman to lust after her hath committed adultery with her already in his heart" (Matthew 5:28, KJV). Therefore, don't allow filthy thoughts to pollute your mind.

The whole issue of lust is involved in the mind or your desires. Some men dream of money and lust for "things." Some women watch soap operas to lust after illicit happiness.

You are supposed to have a clean mind (see 2 Corinthians 10:4-5; 11:3); therefore, guard your thoughts. This doesn't mean you won't be tempted with impure imaginations. A great evangelist once explained,

"You can't be responsible if birds fly over your head, but it is your fault if they lodge in your hair."

As a man "thinketh in his heart, so is he" (Proverbs 23:7, KJV). Before Eve sinned by eating the forbidden fruit, "the woman saw that the tree was good for food ... pleasant to the eyes ... desired to make one wise" (Genesis 3:6). Sin got to her through her mind.

Paul recognized the sources of temptation. "But I fear, lest by any means, as the serpent beguiled Eve through his subtlety, so your minds should be corrupted from the simplicity that is in Christ" (2 Corinthians 11:3). The first step toward sin is usually when our minds think about the act of sin.

4. Do not defile your body.

Some people have the attitude, "My soul lives forever; ignore the body." As a result, they may indulge in drugs, or stink it up like a tobacco barn, or pickle it in alcohol. You cannot separate your body from your soul. The way you treat your body reflects your attitude toward spiritual things, i.e., your soul and eternal life.

The little child stamps his feet, "I can do what I want." Yet the parent knows if he/she plays with matches he/she might burn him/herself. Some may smoke pot to experience the relief of pressure when faced with tension, but the experience may bring more tension, and ultimately a habit some cannot break.

5. Don't link yourself with those who will cause you to stumble.

Your friends are important; they influence your outlook on life. You will have both saved and unsaved friends. You may even have some friends with bad habits, or sin in their life. The issue is "linking" yourself and your way of life to those who will cause you to sin. Therefore, the Bible warns, "Be ye not unequally yoked together with unbelievers" (2 Corinthians 6:14, KJV).

This doesn't mean we should not work at the same job with non-Christians or join the same club. No! We live in a culture where we are with all types of people, in all types of activities. It does mean you should not link yourself in marriage with a person living in obvious sin or link yourself to any commitment where their decisions will determine your Christian life.

The Bible teaches separation from people who have the potential for destroying your life and faith. "Come out from among them, and be ye separate, saith the Lord, and touch not the unclean thing; and I will receive you, and will be a Father unto you, and ye shall be my sons and daughters" (2 Corinthians 6:17-18, KJV). Don't link yourself with those who will pull you down.

6. Do not negatively influence others.

When Cain killed Abel, he asked, "Am I my brother's keeper?" Many have repeated that question, implying they are not responsible for others. But we must be careful not to negatively influence others so that they will sin, or turn against God.

John Donne described, "No man is an island ...." We live in a human community where every action is both influenced by and has an impact on others. We can't isolate ourselves and we must be friends with all kinds of people.

The Bible uses the phrase "stumbling block" to teach that we must not harm others by our sinful influence. If you saw a blind person, or someone with impaired sight, walking, you would never stick out your foot to trip them up. Paul warns, "Take heed lest by any means this liberty of yours become a stumbling block to them that are weak" (1 Corinthians 8:9, KJV).

In many New Testament villages the meat sold in butcher shops had first been sacrificed to idols. New Christians who had previously worshipped idols refused to eat the meat because it was a compromise of their convictions. If they ate meat sacrificed to idols, it suggested they were recognizing the legitimacy of the idol or were returning to idol worship. However, a few Christians thought hamburger was hamburger, ignoring the convictions of the other Christians. They ate meat sacrificed to idols.

Paul stated his opinion: "Neither, if we eat, are we the better; neither, if we eat not, are we the worse" (1 Corinthians 8:8). However, Paul thought it was wrong to hurt others by what he ate. "If meat make my brother to offend, I will eat no flesh" (1 Corinthians 8:13). As a Christian do not do questionable things that may make another stumble into sin.

7. Be careful of little things.

Recently a man's car began to sputter and lose its power. The mechanic checked out the spark plugs, fuel pump, and distributor; still he couldn't find the problem. Finally the mechanic blew out the fuel line. A little bit of trash was causing the problem. There was not enough grit to fill a quarter of a teaspoon, yet it was enough to make the car lose its power.

Sin is like trash in the fuel line. It makes you lose power to obey God and you fall into bad habits. Sin makes you irritable and keeps you from doing what you know is right. Eventually it makes you do wrong for a big way.

LEARN TO LIVE A RIGHTEOUS LIFE

A teenage girl stood on the ledge of a burning building. She was scared and yelled for help. Finally the firemen and their truck arrived. The fireman extended the ladder but could not get any closer to her than a handclasp. The fireman yelled,

"Grab my arm, and I'll grab you ... jump and trust me."

Victory over sin has the same two ingredients as saving the girl from the burning building. First you must leave sin, and second, jump into God's arms.

You can't keep rocking in a chair and pray for God to take away the dizziness you get from rocking. You must leave the rocking chair. God expects believers to live separated *from* sin and separated unto righteousness. It is not enough that you quit sinning; you must do the things that lead to godliness. This is also called victory-living life. It is the basis of living a successful Christian life.

LET THE INDWELLING CHRIST GIVE YOU VICTORY

What is the one thing that separates Christianity from all the other religions of the world? They all claim you can have access to God, but Christianity brings God to you—the Son of God will come live in your life, i.e., "Christ lives in me" (Galatians 2:20, NLT). Yes, other religions claim they offer eternal life with God after death, but Christianity offers life with God immediately at salvation. "I live in this earthly body by trusting in the Son of God who loved me and gave Himself for me" (Galatians 2:20, NLT).

LET YOUR NEW POSITION IN CHRIST GIVE YOU VICTORY

The apostle Paul writes the phrase "in Christ" 216 times, and the apostle John uses it 26 times. It is the basis for New Testament transformation of the individual Christian. When you become a believer in Jesus from salvation, you enter a new relationship with Him. You enter into Jesus. What does that mean?

First, it is a synonym for salvation (see Romans 16:7). But more than outward identification, it means you are justified by Christ. That means you stand forgiven before God. Your sins are covered by the blood of Jesus (see Ephesians 1:7) and you are not only forgiven, but "justification" means "just as if you never sinned." Your record is clean (see Romans 3:24-25), and you stand before God with the position of righteousness of Jesus Christ (see 2 Corinthians 5:21).

Your new position in Christ means you were united with Jesus in His death, burial, and resurrection (see Romans 6:3-10). The Bible describes this process as being baptized or placed into Jesus Christ.

So, what should you make of your new position in Christ? Paul tells us that we should recognize what Christ has done for us and live differently by living for Him. "Consider yourselves to be dead to the powers of sin and alive to God through Christ Jesus" (Romans 6:11, NLT). Paul goes on to explain, "Do not let sin control the way you live" (Romans 6:12, NLT). Instead, "Do what is right for the glory of God ... live under the freedom of God's grace" (Romans 6:14).

LET YOUR NEW NATURE
CONTROL YOUR LIFE

Paul said, "Therefore if any man be in Christ, he is a new creature: old things are passed away; behold, all things are become new" (2 Corinthians 5:17). Your new nature is like sap that runs down a dormant tree each spring. The life-giving sap of a tree is like new life pushing off the dead leaves.

Your old habits are like old leaves. A program to "say no" is not enough. Counting to ten when you get angry is not God's way of victory. You have a new nature; let it flow. Yield to Christ living your new life.

But that's hard because you still have your old sinful nature. Your distaste for the things of the world will grow as you acquire a new taste for spiritual things. Your taste for some habits will change immediately, while others will take longer to appear.

Even though I wasn't yet a Christian, I attended a Sunday evening youth meeting as a junior boy. On several occasions we had a consecration service designed to *purify our lives*. We wrote our sins on small slips of paper then deposited them in a metal dish. After prayer, a candle ignited the paper, and my sins were supposedly purified by fire. I would say, "There it goes, God!"

I always wrote "cursing" on my paper. I tried not to curse for a few days, but I always went back to filthy speech. On one occasion I stood before a campfire and publicly told my friends I would quit cursing.

Two weeks later, as I was cutting open the wire that bundled the papers to deliver on my news route, the wire broke and I gashed my knuckle. I cursed. My friend Art Winn made fun of my empty promise. I couldn't keep my mouth clean before I was saved. But I can testify to the glory of God, I have never cursed since. This does not mean I am perfect, of course, only that God gave me victory over that sin.

SHOW GRATITUDE TO GOD FOR WHAT CHRIST HAS DONE FOR YOU

Paul wrote, "And whatsoever ye do in word or deed, do all in the name of the Lord Jesus, giving thanks to God and the Father by him" (Colossians 3:17, KJV). You dishonor Christ if you continue to live in your old sinful habits. The Bible calls our unsaved state "children of disobedience" (Ephesians 2:2). If you cannot thank Christ for something you do, you had better avoid it. Show appreciation to God for what He has done for you. Let your gratitude guide your actions.

RECOGNIZE THE DANGERS AND MISERIES THAT SIN BREEDS

A professor was rushed to the hospital with stomach cramps, but tests revealed nothing. A month later the entire family went to the emergency room with the same symptoms. Again they could find nothing.

A friend with whom they had gone to Mexico phoned to tell them the source of their problem. They had both bought pottery that was not properly kiln dried. When they poured hot water into the clay pot, its lead paint melted into the hot chocolate, which caused stomach pain.

Although improperly fired pottery is not a sin, the same principle applies. What may seem like a slight sin may affect you, or in the case of my friend, it affected their family. What may seem like a slight sin can cause severe problems to you, or even your family.

Of course we can't get every evil influence out of our life; we live in an evil world. But separating ourselves from sinful practices whenever possible is a step toward godliness. You can't live in a world without sin, but remember the promise that Jesus prayed: "I pray not that thou shouldest take them out of the world, but that thou shouldest keep them from the evil" (John 17:15, KJV).

LIVE RIGHT BY MAINTAINING A STRONG TESTIMONY FOR CHRIST

After I was saved, I was worried some of my friends would drag me back into my old ways. *How can I keep myself clean?* I thought. I told one high school buddy I was sorry for the things we had done together before my salvation. He never came around me again. My positive testimony was enough to keep me from returning to my old ways.

A few days later I talked with a friend who challenged me to a game of pool. He wanted us to go to a "recreation room" to play a game, explaining, "It's not called a pool room anymore." But it had a bar, alcoholic drinks, and a questionable reputation.

"I cannot do that," I answered. "If anyone sees me there, what will they think of me?" I had told them God called me to full-time ministry. I was going to be a preacher.

The Bible demands that we "abstain from all appearance of evil" (1 Thessalonians 5:22). Paul said, "I wrote unto you in an epistle not to company with fornicators ... or with the covetous, or extortioners, or with idolaters ... with such an one no not to eat" (1 Corinthians 5:9-11, KJV).

Believers have to maintain contact with sinners and backsliders in order to be a witness to them, but intimate association with them in questionable activities is discouraged. I could go in a "recreational room" to witness for Christ, but not for pleasure. Later, I played pool in the home of a Christian, also in recreation rooms of Christian institutions.

Conclusion

FIVE TRUTHS ABOUT TEMPTATION

You will not be tempted to sin with any greater enticement than any other believers have faced, but you can be victorious over your temptation. Remember, God is faithful and will not let you be tempted beyond your ability to resist it. He will always make a way to endure it without yielding to it.

1 Corinthians 10:13, ELT

WEBSTER'S definition of "temptation": "to induce or persuade by enticement or allurement." Notice that there are two aspects to temptation. First is the strong external sense of allurement or enticement that comes from the source of the temptation. But the second aspect is internal and has to do with pleasing, gratifying, or satisfying the person. Again, this is the lust of the flesh, the lust of the eyes, or the pride of life (see 1 John 2:16).

FIVE THINGS ABOUT TEMPTATION

1. Temptation is not from God.

When you are tempted to sin or give in to an evil desire, remember what the Bible says: "Let no one say when he is tempted, 'I am tempted by God'; for God cannot be tempted by evil, nor does He Himself tempt anyone" (James 1:13). Therefore, you can never justify temptation by saying this is something good God wants you to have or it is something that comes from God. No, temptation is not from God.

2. Temptation is from satan.

The Bible teaches, "Your adversary the devil walks about like a roaring lion, seeking whom he may devour" (1 Peter 5:8). You may not see the devil or hear the devil, or even come in contact with the devil, but remember, he has great knowledge about sin, how to use sin for his purpose, and how to direct temptation toward us. He also has accumulated knowledge about you. Therefore, the devil will come after you with temptation. The analogy today is that he is like a roaring lion. Remember, a lion is hungry; it is seeking something to eat to satisfy its hunger. The devil, like a hungry lion, is seeking to destroy another animal—you—and eat it. That is a picture of satan's desire to destroy you and eat you alive.

3. Temptation through your sinful nature.

How does temptation get to you? Everyone who is saved has a new nature that will focus their desires toward God. But you also have an old nature; that is the one where temptation focuses you to sin, and it will destroy you.

Paul describes these two natures: "Put off, concerning your former conduct, the old man which grows corrupt according to the deceitful lusts" (Ephesians 4:22). Therefore, we must be wise about our old nature so that it does not destroy us. Then Paul describes "that you put on the new man which was created according to God, in true righteousness and holiness" (Ephesians 4:24). That new man or new nature will point you toward God. It will focus on your obedience to God and worship Him only.

4. Temptation is designed to destroy you.

"Temptation ... when desires have conceived it gives birth to sin, and when sin is full-grown, brings death" (James 1:14-15). Therefore satan knows the weakness of each person and knows each one has an old nature, so he uses these two forces to destroy you.

When temptation is avoided, you can be successfully drawn to Jesus Christ. James writes to us, "Blessed is the man who endures temptation; for when he has been approved, he will receive the crown of life which the Lord has promised to those who love Him" (James 1:12).

5. God has provided for your victory over temptation.

He will not give you victory unless you claim it. The phrase "a way to escape" is a nautical term that comes from sailing the sea during a storm. When you are in the storm, what are you looking for? You are looking for a safe harbor, some place to get away from the storm. So Paul is saying that when you are going through the storms of temptation and trials, God has a safe harbor for you. This means that God can enable you to land safely at the place where you are going.

Quick note: He did not take away the temptation, nor did He take away the storm. What God gives you is the assurance that you can endure the storm until you make it to a harbor.

Look at the phrase "able to bear it." Paul has shown that temptation is serious; more than that, it is life-threatening and debilitating. But when you face the harshest temptation, remember that God makes it possible for you to "bare it."

God does not take away the storm, nor does God want you to act as though there is no storm. God wants you to be realistic about the storm, and He will give you grace in the storm to bear it.

PART TWO

TEMPTATION OVERCOMERS

DEVOTIONS

Day 1

SPIRITUAL WARFARE

But I fear, lest somehow, as the serpent deceived
Eve by his craftiness, so your minds may be
corrupted from the simplicity that is in Christ.

2 Corinthians 11:3

EVE did not recognize that satan/the devil was approaching her in the form of a serpent. She was spiritually blind, i.e., "the god of this world has blinded the minds" (2 Corinthians 4:4). Because we are spiritually blinded like Eve, we must protect ourselves by praying for enlightenment or understanding. "The eyes of your understanding being enlightened that you may know"(Ephesians 1:8). That ought to be a regular prayer request for your quiet time, that God would open your spiritual eyes to recognize and understand spiritual attacks from the enemy. Remember, "The devil walks about like a roaring lion seeking whom he may devour" (1 Peter 5:7). Don't be naive; he is coming after you.

> *Lord, give me spiritual eyes to see and understand evil temp-*
> *tation, then give me wisdom and strength to resist and live*
> *for You. But I need more than protection. I need to grow in-*
> *wardly to be strong in Christ. Amen.*

One of satan's weapons is deception, so be smart about temptation. So put on the full armor of God to protect yourself (see Ephesians

6:10-18). Whether we like it or not, the Christian life is warfare and we must be ready to defend ourselves at all times, and in all ways. Since we face spiritual warfare, we must seek spiritual weapons to defend ourselves and always be alert.

Lord, I will listen to the Holy Spirit, who wants me to be holy, so He warns me about evil and its temptations. Give me ears to listen to Him, and give me a mind to prepare myself for spiritual warfare. Amen.

READING:

Ephesians 6:10-18;

1 Peter 5:8-10;

James 4:1-8

Day 2

THREE GATEWAYS

When the woman saw that the tree was
good for food, that it was pleasant to the
eyes, and a tree desirable to make one wise,
she took of its fruit and ate. She also gave
to her husband with her, and he ate.

Genesis 3:6

Do not love this world nor the things it offers
... a craving for physical pleasure, a craving
for everything we see, and pride in our
achievements and possessions. These are not
from the Father, but are from this world.

1 John 2:15-16, NLT

EVE was tempted in three areas of her life to eat the forbidden fruit. First, the fruit appealed to the lust (or desire) of the flesh; she saw it was "good for food" (Genesis 3:6). She had not yet eaten that fruit and wanted to see how it tasted. Second, she saw "it was pleasant to the eyes" (v. 6). The eyes bring the outside world in to our attention, and Eve wanted something she had never tasted. Finally, Eve realized the fruit was "desirable to make one wise" (v. 6). That desire to enhance one-self appealed to her pride. Here in the first temptation, satan appealed to the total power of personality that opened up the *three gateways* by which temptation gets to us.

> *Lord, help me guard my desires so I don't sin against You by fulfilling my inner lust. Give me wisdom to know Your will and to know my weaknesses. Give me strength to recognize temptation and resist it. Amen.*

Temptation gets to us with wrong/sinful things that appeal to our human personality. You need spiritual wisdom from the Holy Spirit to know yourself and know the nature of temptation. You need inner strength to say no to that which is wrong, and to say yes to that which is right. You need the guidance of the Scriptures ... the inner leading of the Holy Spirit ... the indwelling Christ ... all to keep you safe.

> *Lord, I will study the Bible to learn the right things You want me to do and the wrong things to resist. I need the Holy Spirit to guide me and Your presence to empower me. Amen.*

READING:

1 John 2:1-29

Day 3

DON'T GET INTO AN ARGUMENT WITH SATAN

And the woman said to the serpent, "We may eat the fruit of the trees of the garden; but of the fruit of the tree which is in the midst of the garden, God has said, 'You shall not eat it, nor shall you touch it, lest you die.'"

Genesis 3:2-3

SATAN came to Eve with a question that made her doubt. "Has God said" (Genesis 3:1). She tried to debate with satan, but in her answer she got three things wrong. First she added to what God said: "nor touch it." God did not say that. So when you read the Word of God, do not add to the Bible anything that is not there. Second she altered God's Word; she said, "lest you die" (3:3). God had told Adam, "you shall surely die" (2:17). Her answer to satan was not accurate. Eve altered it to say "lest." Then the third thing Eve did, she omitted something God said. She did not say, "in the day." Eve got into trouble by not accurately quoting God's Word. Don't fall into that trap.

Lord, I will study Your Word carefully to understand everything You have told me to do. May I never add to Your Word what You did not say. May I never alter anything in the Bible. May I never omit anything You say. Amen.

Just as satan got Eve to doubt what God had said, you can fall into that same trap if you don't carefully read and obey the Word of God. Satan wants you to doubt God and deny His Word just as satan did when he originally fell from Heaven. So learn from the negative example of Eve's and then Adam's sin. Know God's Word, live by God's Word, and when you learn the Bible, it will give you eternal life (see John 6:68; Hebrews 4:12).

Lord, I love the song I learned in Sunday school as a child: "Jesus loves me this I know, for the Bible tells me so." Yes, I believe what the Bible says, and I know You love me. Amen.

READING:

John 3:1-36

Day 4

DOUBT

The LORD God took the man ... saying... the tree of knowledge of good and evil you shall not eat.

Genesis 2:15-17

The serpent ... said to the woman, "Has God said you shall not eat ..."

Genesis 3:1

THE Christian life is obeying Jesus when He invites us to "follow Him." Then its obeying what He tells us to do. God made the Christian life as simple as obedience. But the serpent/satan tries to mix up that simple Christian-life formula of obeying the Word of God. Satan does not outrightly attack God at first. Why? Because he knows he will ultimately lose. So satan places doubt in the mind of God's followers. "Has God said?" That doubt creates uncertainty in the minds of God's followers. It makes them question their ability to hear clearly ... their ability to recognize the words and understand them ... the ability to think God's ideas and come to a logical conclusion. So doubt is a very small trick of satan, but it is dangerous ... deadly ... and devilish.

Lord, help me read the Word of God and clearly understand what You want me to do and what You want me to become. Give me a clear mind to see words, understand sentences, and know what You are saying. Protect me from satan's tool of doubt. Amen.

Satan just asked one question to get Eve to think things out for herself and not obey the direction from God. He was able to put doubt in her mind; doubt was the beginning of the first sin. God knows what He wants you to do and become. Satan is smart enough to try to get you to do the very opposite of what God says. He gets into your thinking with doubt.

Lord, help me think my thought after You're through. I will study the Scriptures to know Your plans for me. I will learn Your Word and memorize Your Word and live by the principles of the Bible . I have confidence in the Bible—not doubt. Amen.

READING:

Genesis 3:1-24

Day 5

CLEAR INSTRUCTIONS

The LORD God took the man ... saying, the tree
of the knowledge of good and evil you shall not eat,
for in the day you eat of it you shall surely die.

Genesis 2:15, 17

GOD was very clear about the tree of knowledge of good and evil. He did not want Adam to eat from it. Two things: first, they could eat the fruit from all the other trees in the garden, but they must not eat fruit from that specific tree. God even called the name of the fruit "good and evil" so that there would be no mistake. And second, they would die if they ate its fruit. God had breathed into Adam's nostrils to give him life. Now Adam was to enjoy his new life, and when hungry, he could eat of all the other trees in the garden. Adam also was given the task of keeping the garden. Since weeds, pestilence, and sickness came with the fall of Adam into sin, then his task of keeping the garden must have been relatively easy.

Lord, thank You for creating Earth and putting a garden
with fruit for Adam. I thank You for fruit You have given
me to eat in this life. Thank You for life. Thank You for Your
laws of nature that grow things for me to eat. Amen.

Adam was a personality with *intelligence* (he knew what God meant), *emotions* (desires to eat what was enjoyable and sustain his physical life), and *will* (make free choices). He could choose any other tree, but he didn't. Adam chose to disobey God and please himself, doing what he wanted to do. What can we learn from Adam about choices? Freedom? Disobedience? Consequences?

> *Lord, if I had been in Adam's place, I would have done the same thing. I was born a sinner, and I have sinned. Forgive me, cleanse me by the blood of Jesus Christ, and give me eternal life so I can live with You in Heaven. Amen.*

READING:

Genesis 2:1-25

Day 6

HALF-TRUTH

Then the serpent said to the woman,
"You will not surely die."

Genesis 3:4

WHEN the serpent/satan was talking/tempting Eve, he used a half-truth to blind her eyes to the whole truth. God had told Adam not to eat the fruit of the tree of knowledge of good and evil. "For the day you eat of it, you will surely die" (Genesis 3:17). What did God mean when he said "die"? The word "death" means separation and has a twofold meaning. First, physical death when the soul within the person is separated from the physical body at death. The body goes in the earth and the soul goes to meet God. But there is a second meaning to die or death. It is permanent separation of the human soul from the presence of God where the person is cast into hell for all eternity. "Cast into the lake of fire. This is the second death" (Revelation 20:14).

Lord, I know one day I will die that first death. My physical body will be buried here on Earth and I will come to meet You in Heaven. Thank You for saving me when I accepted Jesus Christ as my Savior. Amen.

When satan told Eve "you will not surely die," he deceived her. Satan meant she would not immediately die physically from eating the fruit. That was a half-truth, meaning she would not drop dead with the first bite. The other half of the truth was eternal death. When Adam and Eve ate the fruit, they died spiritually, meaning they were separated from God. Read the next lesson to see how they received eternal life.

Lord, I believe the Bible. Everyone will die physically (Hebrews 9:27). If a person is not born again (John 3:1-8) and given eternal life by You, they will go to hell, which is the second death. Amen.

READING:

Revelation 20:1-15

Day 7

CLOTHED

*Also for Adam and his wife the Lord God
made tunics of skin, and clothed them.*

Genesis 3:21

*Then I [God] killed an animal sacrifice and brought
its skins to clothe the man and the woman. It
represented the death of an animal and blood which
I require for cleansing to regain fellowship with Me.*

Genesis 3:21, BBJ

THE second quotation above is from *The Bible by Jesus*, a paraphrase of Scriptures that not only contains the words of Scripture but also interprets the verses along with its renditions. *The Bible by Jesus* gives the explanation by Christian scholars throughout history that God came to Adam and Eve after their sin to kill an animal (probably a lamb) in prediction of Jesus's death as the Lamb of God. Then God took the skins of the animal to cover their nakedness. Remember, after their sin Adam and Eve realized they were naked and clothed themselves with leaves. This is a picture of God coming to you and me to forgive our sins and give us fellowship with him.

Lord, thank You for cleansing the sins of Adam and Eve, and thank You for cleansing me. I stand forgiven in the grace of Jesus and I am clothed in His righteousness (2 Corinthians 5:21). Amen.

Go back to that picture of God clothing Adam and Eve with the skin of an animal. That is a picture of God clothing us with the righteousness of Jesus Christ. Remember, Jesus is presented as the Lamb of God. So when we stand in Heaven, we will be as perfect as Jesus, we will be as righteous as He, because we will be clothed in His righteousness.

Lord, another benefit of Heaven is standing there clothed by the righteousness of Jesus Christ. He is my Savior from sin, my indwelling power to live for You. He will be my righteousness when I enter Heaven. Amen.

READING:

Romans 5:1-21

Day 8

BECAUSE OF LOVE

*Again, the devil took Him up on an exceedingly high
mountain, and showed Him all the kingdoms of
the world and their glory. And he said to Him, "All
these things I will give You if You will fall down and
worship me." Then Jesus said to him, "Away with
you, Satan! For it is written, 'You shall worship the
Lord your God, and Him only you shall serve.'"*

Matthew 4:8-10

WHY did Jesus come to Earth as a man, suffer, and ultimately die for the world? Jesus wanted to save people from their sins because He loves them (see John 3:16). But Jesus also wanted to have the people of the world worship and praise Him because He is the Creator-God. Satan offered Jesus a way to get the people of the world to worship Him but look carefully. Satan's plan included no suffering on the cross and no death. Satan thought that Jesus might want an easy way to get the kingdoms of the world without the suffering of the cross. Satan was brilliant in his deceptive offer to Jesus. But Jesus is God; He knows all things. The suffering of the cross was predicted in the Old Testament. Jesus knew that. But He also knew saving lost humanity came only by His suffering on the cross for the world—for me!

Lord Jesus, thank You for refusing the offer of the kingdoms by satan. Thank You for going through the suffering of the cross for me. Thank You for shedding Your blood to cleanse my sins. I thank You, and I worship You! Amen.

Jesus's answer was perfect: "Away with you ... you shall worship the LORD your God and Him only shall you serve" (Matthew 4:10). That needs to be your answer when satan tempts you to sin—any sin; tell the devil you worship the LORD your God and serve Him. Then, after you worship Him for giving you victory over temptation, begin serving Him.

Lord Jesus, thank You for Your example of Your answer to satan when he tempted You to sin. Thank You for Your victory, and I praise You in advance for giving me victory over my next temptation. I will not boast in victory but humbly say thank You and I love You! Amen.

READING:

Matthew 4:1-17

Day 9

HE KNOWS

*For since He [Jesus] Himself has now been
through suffering and temptation, He knows
what it is like when we suffer and are tempted,
and He is wonderfully able to help us.*

Hebrews 2:18, TLB

ONE of the most comforting phrases to help you when you are tempted is "He knows." Jesus was completely God, and we know that "God cannot be tempted with evil" (James 1:13). But Jesus was also completely human, so the Bible is accurate when it declares, "The tempter came to Him" (Matthew 4:3). Yes, Jesus not only was tempted, but the Bible says He "suffered" because of His temptation. Yes, Jesus was hungry and wanted bread to eat. He was tempted. Yes, Jesus wanted people to accept Him as a miracle worker and let angels rescue Him. But Jesus was also God; He was the God-Man. That is a mystery to us humans, but Jesus knows Himself and understands Himself. We are humans worshipping Him.

> *Lord Jesus, I bow at Your feet. You are the Creator-God of eternity. I worship and glorify Your deity. But I also know You are Man—fully Man—who understands me. I accept both and worship You as the God-Man. Amen.*

So be encouraged! When you are tempted and you want to give in, remember, "He knows." When you are tempted and feel like doing it, He knows. When you are discouraged ... He knows. How do you feel today? He knows!

Lord Jesus, You know me because You were tempted, just as much as I am tempted. I get strength from the fact that You know. When I am tired and discouraged ... You know. Amen.

READING:

Hebrews 2:1-18

Day 10

JESUS KNOWS

*Then the devil took Him up into the holy city, set
Him on the pinnacle of the temple, and said to
Him, "If You are the Son of God, throw Yourself
down. For it is written: 'He shall give His angels
charge over you,' and, 'In their hands they shall bear
you up, Lest you dash your foot against a stone.'"*

Matthew 4:5-6

ONE of the evils of satan is pride; he is selfish in seeking the praise
of others. Because of satan's nature, he thought Jesus would be
motivated to seek the praise of the people in the Temple when
they saw Him fall from the pinnacle of the Temple and then in the nick
of time the angels rescuing Him. But Jesus doesn't need satan's help,
nor does Jesus want it. Jesus answered, "you shall not tempt the LORD
your God" (v. 7). Was Jesus telling the devil He didn't want to tempt the
Father? Or did Jesus mean satan shall not tempt Him—Jesus—because
He was the LORD God? Jesus probably meant both. God would never
be glorified with any actions suggested by satan.

*Jesus, thank You for answering satan and pointing out that
it is wrong to tempt God. LORD, give me clear thinking
when I am tempted so I will know how to answer satan's
temptation. Amen.*

Satan was trying to get Jesus to worship him and treat him as deity. But Jesus is omniscient, He knows all things, and He knows the evil suggestions of satan because Jesus is eternal. He existed before the beginning (see Genesis 1:1) and knows satan's devices. So Jesus answered, "you shall not tempt the LORD your God" (v. 7). In His answer, Jesus demonstrated that He knew the evil game satan was trying to play on Him.

> *Jesus, I worship You as the God of creation, and I praise Your wisdom as the LORD of the universe. When I am tempted by satan, give me Your wisdom to see satan's suggestions. Give me an answer of what to do. Give me strength—Your strength—to withstand temptation. Amen.*

READING:

Luke 4:1-15

Day 11

FASTING

*Now when the tempter came to Him, he
said, "If You are the Son of God, command
that these stones become bread."*

Matthew 4:3

WHEN will you be tempted the most: when you are spiritually low or when you are spiritually high? Jesus spent 40
days fasting. But remember, fasting is not primarily about
giving up food; it is about spending time with God the Father. Jesus
had just spent 40 days seeking fellowship with the Father. I think Jesus
was rejoicing as He spent that time with His heavenly Father. I think
He was spiritually ready to begin the mission He was sent to Earth to
accomplish. Satan came to tempt Jesus when He was eager and ready to
do what the Father sent Him to accomplish. What about you? Are you
tempted when you are spiritually strong or spiritually weak? Why not
learn from Jesus. Be ready all the time, at any time. Why? "Because your
adversary the devil walks about like a roaring lion seeking whom he may
devour" (1 Peter 5:8).

*Lord, I will be ready to resist the devil all the time. When I
feel weak and vulnerable, I will be ready. When I am strong,
I will be ready. That is because I will keep in close contact
with You. Amen.*

Jesus, I will fast—just as You fasted—to see the Father working in me and ministering through me. When I am fasting, I am in fellowship with You, and when I finish fasting, I look for You to work in my life, or help me do my work for You in my family, my church, and my work place.

Jesus, thank You for Your example of fasting. Because You are God, You did not need to fast. But I fast to know You better and to serve You more effectively. Also, I will fast to defeat any temptation thrown at me. Amen.

READING:

1 Peter 5:1-14

Day 12

MEMORIZE THE BIBLE

Now when the tempter came to Him, he said, "If You are the Son of God, command that these stones become bread."

Matthew 4:3

SATAN approached Jesus with a compliment when he said, "If you are the Son of God." The Greek language suggests satan was not doubting Jesus's deity but recognizing it. Did satan begin with a compliment to try to throw Jesus off track? We don't know satan's motive, but immediately Jesus answered satan by quoting Scripture: "man shall not live by bread alone" (Deuteronomy 8:3). When you are tempted, follow Jesus's example—quote Scripture. First, the verse you quote will give you strength and courage, but also the Bible will throw satan's plans off track. Remember, the words of the Bible are life and truth (see Hebrews 4:12); quoting the Bible will reinforce God's presence in your life. Isn't that what you need when temptation comes at you?

Jesus, I will read and study the Bible so I will know how to use it when tempted by the devil. I will memorize Bible verses and meditate on them to keep Your presence in my life. Thank You for the Bible. Amen.

When satan showed Jesus the stones, he knew that Jesus was God and could turn them into bread. After all, satan knew Jesus created the world and everything in it (see Colossians 1:16). Also, satan knew that Jesus was hungry. But Jesus answered not with a miracle creation of bread but with a rejection of satan and his attempt to get Jesus to obey his demonic power.

> *Lord, I will fast for spiritual strength to stand against demonic temptation, and after I fast, I will quote the Bible if I am tempted. I will follow Christ's example. I will glorify Jesus in all I do. Amen.*

READING:

Psalm 119:1-24

Day 13

IF

*If You are the Son of God ... if You are the Son
of God ... All these things I will give You if....*

Matthew 4:3, 6, 9

THREE times satan tempted Jesus using the word "if." In the English language "if" is a conjunction. If you do something (meet a condition), you will receive what is promised. Satan had a plan to defeat Jesus. So the devil proposed a hypothetical offer to Jesus. If Jesus did what satan wanted, it would mean Jesus was obeying satan, and at the same time, satan would have won. He would have mastered Jesus. Satan was cunning. All these things satan offered were actual things Jesus wanted. First, Jesus was hungry and wanted bread. Second, Jesus wanted the multitudes to accept Him as a miracle worker who was saved by angels. Third, Jesus wanted to rule the kingdoms of the world so they would worship Him. But to get these, satan would say, "if You do what I say, You can have these"—if would make satan the boss.

Lord Jesus, thank You for letting satan tempt You, but more importantly, thank You for refusing to give satan what he asked. When I am tempted, give me Your wisdom to see satan's deception. Give me strength to say no. Give me Your presence to turn my attention to You and worship You. Amen.

"If" is a big word, and so much in life hangs on our response. Remember, Jesus said, "*If* anyone desires to come after Me, let him deny himself, and take up his cross daily, and follow Me" (Luke 9:23). So make sure you reject the *if* offered by satan and accept the *if* offered by Jesus. When you accept Jesus' *if*, you will get eternal life with Him.

Lord Jesus, thank You for offering me the opportunity to follow You. You said that if I accept Your challenge, I could follow You. Thank You for the privilege of taking up my cross daily and following You. Amen.

READING:

Luke 9:18-62

Day 14

AFTERWARDS

Then the devil left Him, and behold,
angels came and ministered to Him.

Matthew 4:11

SATAN did his best to trip Jesus up, trying to get Him to sin. Satan tried three different times, with three different appeals to Jesus. But none worked. Jesus listened and answered each time "it is written." Once something is written down, it is clear for all to see ... read ... and understand. Jesus answered satan with the Bible. Isn't that a good way for you to answer the temptations from satan? When you quote the Bible, you are quoting God. It's not your opinion, and it's not what you want—it is what God says and it is what God wants. Because Jesus had answered satan so perfectly, what else could satan do? "The devil left Him" (v. 11).

> *Lord Jesus, there are so many reasons why I love You. But because I am tempted to sin—and I have sinned in the past—I love the way You won the victory over satan's temptations. Come dwell in me always. When I am tempted, give me wisdom how to answer, and give me strength to resist. Amen.*

Look at the passage in Luke's gospel. After the temptation it says, "Now when the devil had ended every temptation, he departed from

Him [Jesus] until an opportune time" (Luke 4:13). That means the devil was not through; he would come back again to tempt Jesus. He will do the same to you. When you say no and win over temptation, he will come back. Therefore, watch out!

Lord Jesus, I will watch out for satan, because I have been hurt in the past by sin and I don't want to be hurt again. Give me wisdom, give me guidance, give me strength, give me victory. Amen.

READING:

Hebrews 4:9–5:10

Day 15

REMEMBER JESUS'S DEATH

Peter stood up and addressed them [early church]. ...
"the Scriptures had to be fulfilled concerning Judas,
who guided those who arrested Jesus...." (Judas had
bought a field with the money he received for his
treachery. Falling headfirst there, his body split open
... the people of Jerusalem ... gave the place the ...
name which means "Field of Blood.") ... the book of
Psalms ... says, "Let someone else take his position."

Acts 1:15-21, NLT

THE early church recognized Judas was the one who betrayed Jesus and they named the place where Judas committed suicide "field of blood." Perhaps they made this recognition to deal with the issue of Jesus's arrest, demonstrating that none of the other disciples were responsible for Jesus's death. That was a good historical way of dealing with the issue; but look at the issue today. You and I are responsible for Jesus's death, because our sins put Jesus on the cross. He died for the world; He died for all. He died for each one! He died for me!

Lord Jesus, thank You for dying for me. While You died for
the world (John 3:16), in Your death You forgave my sins

and reconciled me to God the Father. I am eternally grateful. Amen.

While Jesus died for all the world (see John 3:16), the result of His death—forgiveness—applies only to those who call on Him for salvation (see Romans 10:9-13). It is His blood that forgives any and all sinners who repent and believe in Jesus for salvation (see Ephesians 1:7).

Lord Jesus, thank You for Your eternal love that guided You to die for all. Even though the devil used Judas to betray You and deliver You to be crucified, I know it was my sin that was forgiven at the cross. Amen.

READING:

Ephesians 1:3-14

Day 16

VICTORY TODAY

You will not be tempted to sin with any
greater enticement than any other believers
have faced, but you can be victorious over
your temptation. Remember, God is faithful
and will not let you be tempted beyond your
ability to resist it. He will always make a
way to endure it without yielding to it.

1 Corinthians 10:13, ELT

THE pressure you face from the enticement to sin is not a bigger or heavier enticement than any other believer has had to face. So you can never rationalize it by saying, "I have to give in to my temptation because it is so hard ... harder than anyone else has faced." Why? Because God, who knows all things, said, "Your temptation is not greater." But also, God will give you victory over your temptation if you trust Him. He will always have a way of escape. So face each trial and temptation with faith in God who gives us victory.

Lord, thank You for Jesus who indwells me. I can face any
temptation through the power of Jesus Christ who lives in
me and has promised to give me victory. Thank You for Your
love and watchful care. Amen.

When you face temptation, don't yield to it and sin. Rather, yield to Jesus Christ who gives us strength to overcome any test of our salvation. Why? Because He loves us and wants us to live for Him. Also, because He died for our sins so that they will not have a stronghold on us in this life, and they will not cast us into hell when we die. "Thanks be to God who gives us the victory through our Lord Jesus Christ" (1 Corinthians 15:57).

Lord Jesus, thank You for taking care of my eternal salvation by dying on the cross to forgive all my sins. Also, thank You for daily victory over sin by Your indwelling in my heart and Your power to overcome all temptations and sins. Amen.

READING:

1 Corinthians 15:1-34, 51-57

Day 17

ENDURE TESTING AND TEMPTATION

God blesses those who patiently endure testing and temptation. Afterward they will receive the crown of life that God has promised to those who love him. And remember, when you are being tempted, do not say, "God is tempting me." God is never tempted to do wrong, and he never tempts anyone else. Temptation comes from our own desires, which entice us and drag us away. These desires give birth to sinful actions. And when sin is allowed to grow, it gives birth to death.

James 1:12-15, NLT

WHEN you think you are about to give in to sin, remember, God did not mastermind temptation against you. Your heavenly Father is never tempted, and He will never tempt you. The enticement you face comes from within—from your sinful nature. It is that sinful nature that would send you to hell if you were not saved. Notice three things about today's verses. First, our temptation comes from our own desires. Second, these desires lead to sinful actions. Third, our acts of sin will lead to death. That death is called the "second death," which is eternal punishment in hell (Revelation 21:8). Make sure you are saved and have eternal life because that issue is the most important decision you will ever make.

Lord, thank You for dying for my sins and cleansing me from all trespasses. Thank You for giving me eternal life and forgiveness of sins. Thank You that I am now a "child of God" (John 1:12). But most of all, thank You for living in my heart as a guarantee that I will spend eternity with You in Heaven. Amen.

James challenges us that God will bless us when we patiently endure testing and temptation (1:12). To bless means to "add value." When we successfully overcome temptation, God rewards us according to our faithfulness. But we also get strength against the next temptation that comes; and they will keep coming as long as we live on this earth. So victory over your present temptation will strengthen you against the next temptation.

Lord, thank You for every past victory You have helped me achieve. I praise You for strength, and by faith I trust You for victory over the next temptation I will face. Just as You have given me victory in the past, I thank You for victory now and in the future. Amen.

READING:

Revelation 21:1-27

Day 18

WATCH OUT!

Be sober, be vigilant; because your adversary
the devil walks about like a roaring lion,
seeking whom he may devour.

1 Peter 5:8

WHEN you think about your temptations, or you remember any past sins you have done, remember there is a person who plans your temptation to sin. It is satan, also called the devil. Revelation 12:9 (KJV) reminds us he is the "old serpent ... which deceiveth." So, when you give in to your temptation, it is more than pleasing your selfish desires; it also pleases satan. And why is the devil pleased when you sin? Because you are doing what he first did when he tried to take the place and glory of God for himself. Is that what you are doing when you give in to temptation?

Lord Jesus, give me wisdom when I am tempted to under-
stand the evil desires of satan. But also help me realize the
terrible consequences in my life when I sin. But most all, re-
mind me I am sinning against You and denying Your lead-
ership over my life. Amen.

Yes, it is the person of satan behind every temptation to destroy you. But also remember, the person of Jesus is also behind you. He wants to give you victory, and a peaceful life, and abundant joy as you live for Him. "Thanks be unto God who always causes us to triumph in Christ" (2 Corinthians 2:14). You can overcome temptation by living close to Jesus and letting Him live in you.

Lord Jesus, thank You for every time You have helped me triumph over temptation. May You get all the glory for each victory. I have trusted You for overcoming strength in the past. I will trust You for each future victory over sin and temptation. Amen.

READING:

2 Corinthians 2:1-17

Day 19

WALK IN THE LIGHT

But if we are living in the light, as God is in the light, then we have fellowship with each other, and the blood of Jesus, his Son, cleanses us from all sin. If we claim we have no sin, we are only fooling ourselves and not living in the truth. But if we confess our sins to him, he is faithful and just to forgive us our sins and to cleanse us from all wickedness. If we claim we have not sinned, we are calling God a liar and showing that his word has no place in our hearts.

1 John 1:7-10, NLT

WE are challenged as believers to "walk in the light," which is Jesus Christ. He is the light of the world (see John 8:12), and when we live by the light of Jesus Christ, we can be victorious over sin. But suppose you fall into temptation. What then? First, remember that the blood of Jesus Christ will cover each child of God whether they sin ignorantly or willfully. When you give in to temptation, confess, which means acknowledge your sin and show sorrow to God (see Psalm 51:3). When we repent of our sins, it means we determine never to do it again (see Psalm 51:10). Then we have the promise that God will "forgive us our sins and cleanse us of all unrighteousness" (1 John 1:9). Have you done that today?

Lord Jesus, I come to You with gratitude in my heart that Your blood cleanses me from all sin—sins I ignorantly did. You also forgive and cleanse me when I confess and repent. Amen.

You are challenged to be sober and vigilant "because the devil is walking around you" to get you to sin (1 Peter 5:8). But always remember, the devil is on the outside, and Jesus is in your heart—inside—indwelling you. Jesus has the power to keep you from sin. Have you asked Him to do that? Why don't you remind Jesus to keep you now, and the next time you are tempted?

Lord Jesus, thank You for living in my life and forgiving me of my sins. Thank You for Your presence that gives me joy and peace. Thank You for Your guidance so I can live for You. Thank You for ministry to serve You. Amen.

READING:

Psalm 51:1-19

Day 20

OUR ADVOCATE

*My dear children, I am writing this to you so that
you will not sin. But if anyone does sin, we have an
advocate who pleads our case before the Father. He
is Jesus Christ, the one who is truly righteous. He
himself is the sacrifice that atones for our sins—and
not only our sins but the sins of all the world.*

1 John 2:1-2, NLT

THE Bible tells us to live holy lives for God, and it explains that
the way to do it is "that you sin not" (v. 1). That is tough to do
since we have a sin nature. But God would not tell us what He
expects if He did not give us a way to make it happen. We can do it by
making sure Jesus Christ who lives in us is controlling our lives. Make
Him the Lord of your life. Then you can yield all your time, talent, and
treasures to His control every day, for Him to give you victory all day.
Then we can pray daily the Lord's Prayer: "Lead us not into temptation"
(Matthew 6:11). Next, we put on the whole armor of God to stand
against the plans and temptations of the devil (see Ephesians 6:11).

*Lord, I come to You today asking for Your help to keep me
holy so I don't fall into temptation or sin. I want to live a
pure, holy life. I yield my body to Your control and ask You
to live in me. Amen.*

We can live a victorious life when we plan to do right. We are challenged, "Do not be overcome by evil, but overcome evil with good" (Romans 12:21). So our path to an overcomer's life begins with our determination to live for God, then trusting His power to keep us from sin, and then taking advantage of all the tools of victory God has given us.

Lord, thank You for providing the blood of Christ to forgive my sin—all my sins. Thank You for the indwelling Christ to give me inner strength to resist temptation. Thank You for Your grace and wisdom to know my needs before temptation comes and give me a way of escape for victory. Amen.

READING:

1 John 1:1-2; 2

Day 21

OBTAINING MERCY AND GRACE

Seeing then that we have a great High Priest who has passed through the heavens, Jesus the Son of God, let us hold fast our confession. For we do not have a High Priest who cannot sympathize with our weaknesses, but was in all points tempted as we are, yet without sin. Let us therefore come boldly to the throne of grace, that we may obtain mercy and find grace to help in time of need.

Hebrews 4:14-16

WHEN you are tempted to sin, remember that Jesus was also tempted by satan after He had fasted for 40 days. But Jesus was victorious. When you are tempted, go to Him in prayer. Why? First, Jesus understands when temptation gets to the inner core of your soul. That is because "He was tempted in all points like as we are, yet without sin" (v. 15, ELT). Second, Jesus has given you an example to resist temptation. Each time, Jesus answered satan with "It is written ..." The secret to Jesus's victory over temptation was Scripture. So your answer to victory is also found in Scripture. Third, we can pray to find His mercy, because we are weak. It is then that we find His "help in time of need." We find His victory.

Lord Jesus, I come to You about my temptations, because You are the perfect example of victory over satan's temptations. Also, I come to You because You have the power to stop satan and give me victory. Amen.

Did you see that section where Jesus is concerned with the feeling of your infirmities (v. 15)? Look at that verse again in the New Living Translation: "This High Priest of ours understands our weaknesses, for he faced all of the same testings we do, yet he did not sin" (v. 15). Therefore, Jesus is with you right in the middle of a temptation because He has been there. He will give you victory.

Lord Jesus, You are a wonderful Savior from sin. Thank You for my salvation. Also, You provide a wonderful victory over temptation so we can live for You. Thank You for Your power to live for You. Amen.

READING:

Hebrews 2:16-18; 4:12-14

Day 22

VICTORY-LIVING

Now thanks be to God who always
leads us in triumph in Christ ...

2 Corinthians 2:14

But thanks be to God, who gives us the
victory through our Lord Jesus Christ.

1 Corinthians 15:57

THESE two verses promise that the followers of Jesus Christ will triumph over sin in their lives and that He would give them victory. Since God has promised victory-living, let's claim it daily in our lives. This book promises that you can overcome temptation—let's praise God for that first step in victory-living. But let's go on to daily victory-living. That triumphant lifestyle is based on the indwelling Christ, so let Him live through you to gain victory. But also, yield to the indwelling Christ so that His strength will give you victory and His indwelling presence will give you joy ... peace ... and assurance. There is no better life than when you realize "Christ in you, the hope of glory" (Colossians 1:27).

Lord Jesus, thank You for each victory You have given me to live for You. I want Your presence indwelling me, to be strength over temptation. But more than victory over temptation, I want Your fullness flowing into me and through me. Amen.

When Jesus came into your life, He gave you forgiveness of sins, eternal life, eternal joy, and peace. But more than all that, Jesus gave you His presence. Now, "Christ lives in [you]" (Galatians 2:20), so now you live by His inward power, and His inward love, and His inward guidance. Yes, Jesus does many things for You, but His inward presence is greater than all the things He gives. For when you have Jesus's presence in your life, you have Him (see Philippians 1:21).

Lord Jesus, thank You for all the things You do for me, and thank You for all the things You give me. But most of all, thank You for Your presence in my life. Without You I do not have life, but You are my life ... my everything! Amen.

READING:

Galatians 1:9-29

Day 23

OUR NEW POSITION GIVES US STRENGTH

But God ... loved us, even when we were
dead in [sin], made us alive together with
Christ ... raised us up together, and made
us sit together ... in Christ Jesus.

Ephesians 2:4-6

NEW believers experience the transforming power of God in their lives. Some will experience deeper changes than others, some experience changes quicker than others, and others will grow in their faith stronger than others. But all believers when saved are immediately given a new standing before God. All believers have new life (eternal) in Christ. They have been raised together with Christ into the presence of the Father in Heaven. Also, they have a new position, seated with Christ in the heavenlies. If every new believer could immediately see all they have in Christ, they would immediately put aside the sins in their lives and be motivated to grow in spiritual development and serve Jesus in their new relationship to Him.

Lord Jesus, open my blind eyes to see all You have done for
me, and help me live according to all You have provided for

me, and use me in Your service to accomplish all You want to do through me. Amen.

Many Christians seem to walk around in spiritual poverty when God has given them riches in Heaven. They have a rich new position in Jesus Christ, but they act like beggars. The Bible says, "God who is rich in mercy ... in the ages to come. He might show the exceeding riches of His grace ... toward us in Christ Jesus" (Ephesians 2:4, 7). Our riches in Heaven remind us that "God will supply all our needs according to His riches in glory" (Philippians 4:19).

Lord Jesus, thank You for all You have given me in Christ Jesus. Help me live a positive testimony for Him. I want to serve Him, follow Him, and glorify Him. Help me live on Earth as Your follower, and help me glorify You in all things. Amen.

READING:

Ephesians 2:1-22

Day 24

LOOK TO JESUS

*Therefore, we also, since we are surrounded by so
great a cloud of witnesses, let us lay aside every
weight, and the sin which so easily ensnares us, and
let us run with endurance the race that is set before
us, looking unto Jesus, the author and finisher of
our faith, who for the joy that was set before Him
endured the cross, despising the shame, and has
sat down at the right hand of the throne of God.*

Hebrews 12:1-2

THE secret of overcoming temptation is not in your spiritual strength, nor is it in your knowledge of Christianity or past accomplishments for God. The secret of overcoming is Jesus— look to Him. The next time you are tempted to sin, get your eyes off yourself and off the satisfaction that is enticing you to sin. Get your eyes on Jesus. Remember, the secret to the great heroes of faith is "looking unto Jesus the author of our faith" (Hebrews 12:2). When do you look to Him? Before you are tempted, during the fire of temptation, and after He gives you victory. Because Jesus overcame temptation, He will help you be victorious.

Lord, I realize a lot of temptation comes through my eyes. Help me to look to Jesus, my strength in trouble. Help me see Jesus as my deliverer from temptation. I need You every day. Amen.

To be an overcomer, you have to see the other side of temptation. Sin may be there waiting for you. But also, Jesus is waiting to help you become an overcomer. But more than that, Jesus is indwelling you. "Christ lives in me" (Galatians 2:20). So look to your inner strength in temptation. Look to Jesus who lives in your heart. He was victorious over sin in His life on Earth, and He can make you an overcomer against your temptations.

Jesus, You are my past Savior from sin, and now I am claiming You as my present Savior from any present temptations, and I also claim you as my future Savior from sin who will take me home when I die, or when the rapture comes. Amen.

READING:

Hebrews 11:1–12:2

Day 25

GREAT HEROES

*Now all these things happened to them as examples,
and they were written for our admonition.*

1 Corinthians 10:11

THE stories of great heroes of faith overcoming temptation should do several things for you. First, if they can become an overcomer, then why not you? What would it take for you to be an overcomer? Second, look at the ways they overcame. Not all overcomers do the same things or use the same methods, or even respond at the same time. You may not do it like them, but you can be an overcomer. Maybe you think you don't have the inner ability to overcome. All overcomers started somewhere—so where will you start? They lived among the lost of the world, just as you do. So let's learn from the examples of overcomers, and learn from their faith, and learn from their boldness, and let's ask God to use us as He used them.

> *Lord, I want to be an overcomer. I confess my weaknesses in past failures. Fill me with the power of the Holy Spirit and use me to be an overcomer. I dedicate myself now, and I am ready now. I will start now. Amen.*

Everyone has their own barriers that keep them from overcoming temptation. Everyone has their own challenges where they must serve

God and overcome their weaknesses. Just as everyone in the past had to get started somewhere and/or some place, they had to get started just as you have to get started. When is a good time for you to be an overcomer?

Lord, now is a good time. I am starting now. Redirect my life to serve You. I confess my past failures and ask for Your help in future projects. I will serve You now and in the future. Amen.

READING:

1 Corinthians 10:1-15

Day 26

YOUR CONSCIENCE

Therefore, to him who knows to do good
and does not do it, to him it is sin.

James 4:17

Temptation comes from our own desires, which
entice us and drag us away. These desires
give birth to sinful actions. And when sin is
allowed to grow, it gives birth to death.

James 1:14-15, NLT

AN overcomer begins with what they know. If they know something is wrong but they keep doing it—it is wrong. First, knowing begins with our conscience when it tells you no ... listen to your conscience. Someone said the conscience may not tell us what to do. But if you go against your conscience, you weaken yourself. Your convictions are weakened. Your ability to say no to obvious sins may be weakened. Your whole inner person is weakened. To be a temptation overcomer, listen to your conscience. Not only must your inner self guide you, but it must also have the strength to point you to Jesus Christ. Following Jesus will make you even stronger and wiser than following your conscience.

Lord, I will listen to Jesus and do what He wants me to do. I will not go against His commands, but I will do what He wants me to do, and I will go where He wants me to go, and I will be what He wants me to be. Amen.

You begin to learn yourself when you begin to learn your conscience. Then you begin to grow in your strength and your self-awareness to sin, but especially when you strengthen your self-awareness to God. It is the Lord who will keep you thinking straight, and acting properly, and following His leading in your life.

Lord, I want to be strong inwardly and of course outwardly. I will learn what the Scriptures teach about who You are, and what You do for me, and how You want me to live my life and serve You. I am ready to follow You in every part of my life. Amen.

READING:

Luke 9:23-62

Day 27

NEW CREATION

*Therefore, if anyone is in Christ, he is a
new creation; old things have passed away;
behold, all things have become new.*

2 Corinthians 5:17

ID you see the word "if" that promises that those in Christ are
a new creation, that old things have passed away? "All things
have become new." "If" is a wonderful promise, but to receive
a promise, you have to act on it. First, the condition "if." The unsaved
do not receive new life from Jesus, and they do not get to enjoy the new
life Jesus promises. Have you taken advantage of the conditional "if"?
To receive the promise of a new life, you must be in Christ. That means
believing in His death to forgive your sins and accepting Him into your
life as your Savior. When you receive Christ into your life, you become
a new creation—Christ has given you eternal life and a new beginning
in life.

*Lord Jesus, I ask You to cleanse my sins and save me from
hell. Thank You for eternal life. You brought a new challenge
into my life and thank You for Your indwelling in my heart.
Amen.*

That first word "if" is conditional: you must meet God's conditions to be a Christian. You must repent and turn from your old ways of living, and then realize you cannot save yourself. So you invite Jesus into your life. Because He is the eternal God, He gives you eternal life. Because He lives at the right hand of the heavenly Father, He will take you to Heaven to live with Him when you die.

> *Lord Jesus, I thank You for everything You have given me. I have forgiveness and eternal life, hope, joy, and a purpose in life to serve You. Guide me in my daily life. Amen.*

READING:

2 Corinthians 5:1-21

Day 28

WHAT GRATITUDE REFLECTS

And whatever you do in word or deed, do
all in the name of the Lord Jesus, giving
thanks to God the Father through Him.

Colossians 3:17

O F all the virtues you show to others, people remember when you give them money, things, food, time, and other deeds of mercy. But it seems the old adage is still true: "Gratitude is the least remembered of all virtues, but it is your acid test of character." When you are grateful for big things someone does for you, they appreciate your expression of thanks. But what about little things? Don't let the good things someone does for you slip by unnoticed. Most people just forget those little things. But when you are grateful for both big and little things, it shows that little things are also important in life. Then it shows you appreciate the gift and the giver. But most of all, it shows you live by the principle of appreciation. You recognize them, thank them, and encourage them in their giving attitude.

Lord Jesus, help me appreciate the big and little things peo-
ple give me. But especially help me remember to show appre-
ciation to the person giving to me. Amen.

Why is appreciation important? Because you recognize the person who is giving to you. They took their time ... and effort ... and resources to give to you. You recognize their unselfish moment, and appreciate the sacrifice of their time, resources, and themselves. But most of all, when you express appreciation, your self-worth goes up in your own estimate. Gratitude not only expresses your inner character, it grows and strengthens your inner character.

> *Lord Jesus, make me grateful for all that my parents, friends, and teachers have done for me. Make me grateful for the opportunity and freedom to live for You. But most of all, make me grateful for all You have done for me. Thank You, Lord! Amen.*

READING:

Colossians 3:1-17

PART THREE

TEMPTATION
OVERCOMERS

LESSONS

Lesson 1:

THE CONSEQUENCES OF GIVING INTO TEMPTATION

*Now the serpent was more cunning than any beast
of the field which the Lord God had made. And
he said to the woman, "Has God indeed said, You
shall not eat of every tree of the garden?" And the
woman said to the serpent, "We may eat the fruit
of the trees of the garden; but of the fruit of the
tree, which is in the midst of the garden, God has
said, You shall not eat it, nor shall you touch it,
lest you die." Then the serpent said to the woman,
"You will not surely die. For God knows that in
the day you eat of it your eyes will be opened, and
you will be like God, knowing good and evil."*

Genesis 3:1-5

A. WHAT IS TEMPTATION?

1. Webster's definition: "To **seduce**, entice, or persuade."

   a. The source will **hide** its intent.

   b. The object of temptation—the naïve.

   c. Original meaning—to attract with gratification (i.e., what you are). To do that which is **not intended** or not natural.

2. The serpent/satan wanted Eve to do what he originally did: **deny/ disobey** God.

3. Why target the woman? "Said to the woman" (v. 1). **Stronger** emotions/feelings/sensitivity.

4. Original approach—"Has God said?" (v. 1). Created **doubt**.

5. Webster's meaning of "doubt": "To be uncertain, **hesitant**, questionable." Original: "to fear or to scare."

6. Temptation's threefold strategy:

   a. **Added** to God's Word. "Touch it" (v. 3).

   b. **Altered**. "You shall surely die" (2:17). "Lest you die" (3:3).

   c. **Omitted**. "In the day" (2:17).

7. God told Adam (Genesis 2:15-17):

   a. Did Adam not **communicate** clearly to Eve?

   b. Did Eve not hear and understand?

8. Half-truth: "You will not surely die" (vv. 3-4). Die **spiritually**, not **physically**.

9. Temptation's results:

    a. New awareness/**attractions**, "eyes opened" (v. 5).

    b. b. To understand as **proven**, "knowing good and evil" (v. 5).

B. THREEFOLD TEMPTATION

1. Lust/desire of **flesh**, i.e., physical, "good for food." Needed to continue **physical** life.

2. Lust/desire of **eyes**, i.e., emotional, good for happiness, needed **internal satisfaction**.

3. Lust/desire of **pride**, good to protect or enhance self-**awareness**.

C. CONSEQUENCES

"She took some of the fruit and ate it. Then she gave some to her husband, who was with her, and he ate it." (Genesis 3:6 b, NLT)

1. Awareness of both—knew their spiritual **positive** and physical negative passions.

2. Awareness to "hide" their new **physical passion**. "They knew they were naked" (3:7). They made clothes.

3. **God-consciousness**. "They heard the sound of the LORD God walking ... presence of the LORD God" (3:8).

4. "God called" (3:9). God knew:

    a. **What** they did.

    b. **Where** they were hiding.

    c. **What** He was going to do.

    d. And to fix **responsibly**, "who told you that you were naked?" (v. 7).

5. Pass the buck:

    a. Adam, "The woman You gave me ... I ate" (v. 12).

    b. Eve, "the serpent deceived me" (v. 13).

6. The **serpent**:

    a. "On your belly" (v. 19)

    b. **Conflict**. "And I will put enmity between you and the woman, And between your seed and her Seed; He shall bruise your head, and you shall bruise His heel" (3:15).

    c. Her seed, *proto evangelium* (Latin), **first giving of the gospel**.

7. Eve:

    a. **Pain**. "Sorrows ... bring forth children" (v. 16).

    b. **Submissive**. "You desire ... husband" (3:16).

8. Adam, hard work, "thorns ... sweat ..." (vv. 18-19).

D. TEN LESSONS TO LEARN ABOUT TEMPTATION

1. Satan is the **source of your temptation**. He wants you to do what he did and be punished as he was.

2. Temptation is not **good or positive**, and it intends to harm you.

3. Temptation and its source will appeal to your **weakness**.

4. No one is **above/beyond** temptation in sex, age, spiritual strength, etc.

5. Temptation comes from without and offers you various **enticements** you may want.

6. When attractions are offered, the person is usually not aware of the **consequences** of temptations.

7. Temptations appear in the form of physical enticements, emotional gratifications, or **egotistical** enhancements.

8. The **consequences** of giving in to temptations are absolute.

9. God knows you are human and has a **solution of forgiveness**.

10. It is your responsibility to **confess** your sin, **accept** forgiveness, and **live** in a new relationship to God, and **serve** Him.

Lesson 1:

QUESTIONS

THE CONSEQUENCES OF GIVING INTO TEMPTATION

Now the serpent was more cunning than any beast
of the field which the Lord God had made. And
he said to the woman, "Has God indeed said, You
shall not eat of every tree of the garden?" And the
woman said to the serpent, "We may eat the fruit
of the trees of the garden; but of the fruit of the
tree, which is in the midst of the garden, God has
said, You shall not eat it, nor shall you touch it,
lest you die." Then the serpent said to the woman,
"You will not surely die. For God knows that in
the day you eat of it your eyes will be opened, and
you will be like God, knowing good and evil."

Genesis 3:1-5

A. WHAT IS TEMPTATION?

1. Webster's definition: "To _____ , entice, or persuade."

   a. The source will _____ its intent.

   b. The object of temptation—the naïve.

   c. Original meaning—to attract with gratification (i.e., what you are). To do that which is _____ or not natural.

2. The serpent/satan wanted Eve to do what he originally did: _____ / _____ God.

3. Why target the woman? "Said to the woman" (v. 1). _____ emotions/feelings/sensitivity.

4. Original approach—"Has God said?" (v. 1). Created _____ .

5. Webster's meaning of "doubt": "To be uncertain, _____ , questionable." Original: "to fear or to scare."

6. Temptation's threefold strategy:

   a. _____ to God's Word. "Touch it" (v. 3).

   b. _____ . "You shall surely die" (2:17). "Lest you die" (3:3).

   c. _____ . "In the day" (2:17).

7. God told Adam (Genesis 2:15-17):

    a. Did Adam not _____ clearly to Eve?

    b. Did Eve not hear and understand?

8. Half-truth: "You will not surely die" (vv. 3-4).
    Die _____ , not _____ .

9. Temptation's results:

    a. New awareness/ _____ , "eyes opened" (v. 5).

    b. b. To understand as _____ , "knowing good
        and evil" (v. 5).

B. THREEFOLD TEMPTATION

1. Lust/desire of _____ , i.e., physical, "good for
    food." Needed to continue _____ life.

2. Lust/desire of _____ , i.e., emotional, good for
    happiness, needed _____ .

3. Lust/desire of **pride**, good to protect or enhance
    self- _____ .

C. CONSEQUENCES

"She took some of the fruit and ate it. Then she gave some to her husband, who was with her, and he ate it." (Genesis 3:6 b, NLT)

1. Awareness of both—knew their spiritual _____ and physical negative passions.

2. Awareness to "hide" their new _____ . "They knew they were naked" (3:7). They made clothes.

3. _____ . "They heard the sound of the LORD God walking ... presence of the LORD God" (3:8).

4. "God called" (3:9). God knew:

   a. _____ they did.

   b. _____ they were hiding.

   c. _____ He was going to do.

   d. And to fix _____ , "who told you that you were naked?" (v. 7).

5. Pass the buck:

   a. Adam, "The woman You gave me ... I ate" (v. 12).

   b. Eve, "the serpent deceived me" (v. 13).

6. The _____ :

   a. "On your belly" (v. 19)

   b. _____ . "And I will put enmity between you and the woman, And between your seed and her Seed; He shall bruise your head, and you shall bruise His heel" (3:15).

c. Her seed, *proto evangelium* (Latin),

_____ .

7. Eve:

   a. _____ . "Sorrows ... bring forth children"
   (v. 16).

   b. _____ . "You desire ... husband" (3:16).

8. Adam, hard work, "thorns ... sweat ..." (vv. 18-19).

D. TEN LESSONS TO LEARN ABOUT TEMPTATION

1. Satan is the _____ . He wants
   you to do what he did and be punished as he was.

2. Temptation is not _____ ,
   and it intends to harm you.

3. Temptation and its source will appeal to your _____ .

4. No one is _____ temptation in sex, age, spiritual
   strength, etc.

5. Temptation comes from without and offers you various
   _____ you may want.

6. When attractions are offered, the person is usually not aware of the
   _____ of temptations.

7. Temptations appear in the form of physical enticements, emotional
   gratifications, or _____ enhancements.

8. The _____ of giving in to temptations are absolute.

9. God knows you are human and has a _____ .

10. It is your responsibility to _____ your sin, _____ forgiveness, and **live** in a new relationship to God, and _____ Him.

Lesson 2:

LET JESUS SHOW YOU HOW TO FACE TEMPTATION

Jesus was led by the Spirit into the wilderness to be tempted by the devil ... fasted forty days and forty nights, afterwards ... hungry. The tempter said "if you are the Son of God ... stones become bread. Jesus ... "It is written man shall not live by bread alone, but by every word ... mouth of God." Devil took Him to holy city ... "if you are the Son of God ... throw yourself down, for it is written He shall give His angels charge over You ... they shall bear You up lest You dash Your foot against a stone." Jesus ... "it is written, you shall not tempt the LORD your God." Again, devil ... exceedingly high mountain ... "all this I will give You, if You will fall down and worship me." Jesus ... "it is written, you shall worship the LORD your God and Him only" ... devil left him.

Matthew 4:1-11

A. INTRODUCTION

1. Jesus baptized, fasted, then **immediately was tempted**. Just as Adam was tempted at the first of his ministry, Jesus, the Second Adam, was tempted at the beginning of His ministry (see 1 Corinthians 15:45-47).

2. Forty is the number of testing.

3. The Holy Spirit led Jesus there, but the devil **came to Him** (v. 3).

B. FIRST TEMPTATION—PHYSICAL HUNGER

1. If ... Son of God. *If* is indicative, assuming an **actual fact**. The devil knows **Jesus is God**.

2. As God, Jesus did not need to eat but could do a miracle for food. As a **man**, Jesus was hungry. Devil tries to split **nature of Jesus**.

3. Answer with Scriptures, "**It is written**," i.e., standeth complete.

C. SECOND TEMPTATION— DEMONSTRATE HIS DEITY

1. "The devil taketh," i.e., **leads** to a religious place. Not ten acres of Mt. Zion, but highest point of building.

2. Devil both leaves out and garbles his quote of Bible, Psalm 91:11-12:

   a. **Leaves out** "to keep you in all your ways" (Psalm 91:11).

   b. **Adds** "at any time."

3. "It is written" (Deuteronomy 6:16), "Thou shalt not tempt the LORD thy God" (v. 7).

D. THIRD TEMPTATION—DIVEST HIS POWER AND GIVE TO SATAN

1. "The devil taketh (leads up) ... high mountain" (v. 8). Where? ___ _____.

2. "The devil ... shows Him, kingdoms ... glories" (v. 8). How? _____ _____.

3. "The devil ... says ... all I will give if ... fall down and worship me" (v. 9). Why? _____.

4. Jesus answers with three statements:

   a. "It is written."

   b. "You shall worship the LORD your God, and Him only shall you serve" (v. 10).

   c. "Go." Satan departed.

   In falling, Adam **lost**.

   In victory, Jesus **gained**.

E. TEN PRACTICAL LESSONS FROM JESUS'S VICTORY OVER TEMPTATION

1. Jesus is our **example**; we can trust Him for victory over temptation. "We have a great High Priest ... who was in all points tempted as we are, yet without sin. Let us therefore come boldly to the throne of grace, that we may obtain mercy and find grace to help in time of need" (Hebrews 4:14, 16).

2. Just as the devil aimed **specific temptations** at Jesus, so he will aim certain temptations at your weaknesses.

3. Temptations comes with the "if" quality of **possibility** when aimed at our weakness.

4. Many temptations will come when you are **physically weak,** just as satan tempted Jesus with bread after He had not eaten for 40 days.

5. Some temptations will attempt to get you to **disobey Scripture,** i.e., to go against the written Word of God.

6. Your best defense against temptation is quoting the **written Word of God**. Therefore, learn the Bible, memorize the Bible, and use the Bible.

7. Since the devil tempted Jesus, who was/is satan's **strongest opponent**, you can be sure he will come after you.

8. Just as Jesus answered the devil's temptations and defeated him, the **indwelling** Jesus is your source to defeat satan (see Philippians 1:21; 4:13).

---

9. Just as satan left Jesus but **returned later**, he will do the same to you.

10. When we choose to follow Jesus, we will be tempted just as He was. **Be prepared to win**!

Lesson 2:

LET JESUS SHOW YOU HOW TO FACE TEMPTATION

Jesus was led by the Spirit into the wilderness to be tempted by the devil ... fasted forty days and forty nights, afterwards ... hungry. The tempter said "if you are the Son of God ... stones become bread. Jesus ... "It is written man shall not live by bread alone, but by every word ... mouth of God." Devil took Him to holy city ... "if you are the Son of God ... throw yourself down, for it is written He shall give His angels charge over You ... they shall bear You up lest You dash Your foot against a stone." Jesus ... "it is written, you shall not tempt the LORD your God." Again, devil ... exceedingly high mountain ... "all this I will give You, if You will fall down and worship me." Jesus ... "it is written, you shall worship the LORD your God and Him only" ... devil left him.

Matthew 4:1-11

A. INTRODUCTION

1. Jesus baptized, fasted, then _____ .
   Just as Adam was tempted at the first of his ministry, Jesus, the
   Second Adam, was tempted at the beginning of His ministry (see 1
   Corinthians 15:45-47).

2. Forty is the number of testing.

3. The Holy Spirit led Jesus there, but the devil
   _____ (v. 3).

B. FIRST TEMPTATION—PHYSICAL HUNGER

1. If ... Son of God. *If* is indicative, assuming an _____ .
   The devil knows _____ .

2. As God, Jesus did not need to eat but could do a miracle for food.
   As a **man**, Jesus was hungry. Devil tries to split
   _____ .

3. Answer with Scriptures, " _____ ,"
   i.e., standeth complete.

C. SECOND TEMPTATION—
DEMONSTRATE HIS DEITY

1. "The devil taketh," i.e., _____ to a religious place. Not ten acres of Mt. Zion, but highest point of building.

2. Devil both leaves out and garbles his quote of Bible, Psalm 91:11-12:

   a. _____ "to keep you in all your ways" (Psalm 91:11).

   b. _____ "at any time."

3. "It is written" (Deuteronomy 6:16), "Thou shalt not tempt the LORD thy God" (v. 7).

D. THIRD TEMPTATION—DIVEST HIS
POWER AND GIVE TO SATAN

1. "The devil taketh (leads up) ... high mountain" (v. 8). Where? _____ .

2. "The devil ... shows Him, kingdoms ... glories" (v. 8). How? _____ .

3. "The devil ... says ... all I will give if ... fall down and worship me" (v. 9). Why? _____ .

4. Jesus answers with three statements:

   a. "It is written."

   b. "You shall worship the LORD your God, and Him only shall you serve" (v. 10).

   c. "Go." Satan departed.

      In falling, Adam _____ .

      In victory, Jesus _____ .

E. TEN PRACTICAL LESSONS FROM JESUS'S VICTORY OVER TEMPTATION

1. Jesus is our _____ ; we can trust Him for victory over temptation. "We have a great High Priest ... who was in all points tempted as we are, yet without sin. Let us therefore come boldly to the throne of grace, that we may obtain mercy and find grace to help in time of need" (Hebrews 4:14, 16).

2. Just as the devil aimed _____ at Jesus, so he will aim certain temptations at your weaknesses.

3. Temptations comes with the "if" quality of _____ when aimed at our weakness.

4. Many temptations will come when you are _____ , just as satan tempted Jesus with bread after He had not eaten for 40 days.

5. Some temptations will attempt to get you to _____ , i.e., to go against the written Word of God.

6. Your best defense against temptation is quoting the
_____ . Therefore, learn the
Bible, memorize the Bible, and use the Bible.

7. Since the devil tempted Jesus, who was/is satan's
_____ , you can be sure he
will come after you.

8. Just as Jesus answered the devil's temptations and defeated him, the
Jesus is your source to defeat satan (see Philippians 1:21; 4:13).

9. Just as satan left Jesus but _____ , he will do the
same to you.

10. When we choose to follow Jesus, we will be tempted just as He
was. _____ !

PROTECTION AGAINST TEMPTATION

You will not be tempted to sin with any greater enticement than any other believers have faced, but you can be victorious over your temptation. Remember, God is faithful and will not let you be tempted beyond your ability to resist it. He will always make a way to endure it without yielding to it.

1 Corinthians 10:13, ELT

A. THINGS KNOWN ABOUT TEMPTATION

1. **Not from God**. "Let no one say when he is tempted, 'I am tempted by God'; for God cannot be tempted by evil, nor does He Himself tempt anyone" (James 1:13).

2. From **satan**. "Your adversary the devil walks about like a roaring lion, seeking whom he may devour" (1 Peter 5:8).

3. Through your **sinful nature**. "But each one is tempted when he is drawn away by his own desires and enticed" (James 1:14).

4. Designed to **destroy you**. "Temptation ... when desires have conceived it gives birth to sin, and when sin is full-grown, brings death" (James 1:14-15).

5. Temptation can successfully get to someone **close to Jesus**. "The devil had already put into the heart of Judas Iscariot ... to betray Him" (John 13:2).

B. WHERE WILL SATAN ATTACK?

Do not love the world or the things in the world. If anyone loves the world, the love of the Father is not in him. For all that is in the world—the lust of the flesh, the lust of the eyes, and the pride of life—is not of the Father but is of the world. (1 John 2:15-16)

1. Lust of the flesh—**physical**:

   a. Lust involving things that will **please** the physical body.

   b. This does not include **necessities**, i.e., food, drink, etc.

2. Lust of the eyes, **things**, attractions, money, possessions, clothes, luxuries, hobbies, etc.

3. Pride of life:

   a. Ego **enhancement**, fame, position, etc.

   b. This does not mean ego, strength, confidence, i.e., to know yourself, your strength, your purpose in life, or your positive contribution.

C. WHAT TO DO IF YOU GIVE IN TO TEMPTATION

1. Your goal is to not sin but be as perfect as possible. "These things I write to you, so that you may not sin" (1 John 2:1).

2. Jesus was perfect; you **are not**. Jesus did not give in; **you might**.

   a. No one has a perfect **track record**. "If we say we have not sinned, we deceive ourselves" (1 John 1:8).

   b. Everyone has been **tempted**. "Each one is tempted" (James 1:14).

3. Whenever you sin, remember that you have a Savior who **understands**. "You have a High Priest who can sympathize with your weakness, He was tempted in all points, but did not sin ... come boldly to His throne to obtain mercy and find grace" (Hebrews 4:15-16, ELT).

4. Confess your sins. "If we confess our sins, He is faithful and just to forgive ... and cleanse" (1 John 1:9).

5. Repent and determine not to **do it again**. "Create in me a clean heart, O God, and renew a steadfast spirit within me" (Psalm 51:10).

6. God remembers them **no more** (see Isaiah 43:35; Jeremiah 31:36; Hebrews 9:12; 10:16-17).

D. TEN THINGS GOD PROVIDES TO RESIST TEMPTATIONS

1. **Prepare** with prayer. "Lead me not into temptation but deliver me from the evil one" (Matthew 6:11, ELT).

2. Begin by **yielding** to God. "Submit yourselves therefore to God. Resist the devil, and he will flee from you" (James 4:7).

3. Determine to **resist** and be firm. "Be sober, be vigilant; because your adversary the devil walks about like a roaring lion, seeking whom he may devour" (1 Peter 5:8).

4. **Trust** God for victory. "The Lord knows how to rescue the godly" (2 Peter 2:9).

5. Claim Jesus's **intercession** for you. "For we ... have a High Priest ... let us therefore come boldly to the throne of grace, that we may obtain mercy and find grace to help in time of need" (Hebrews 4:15-16).

6. Follow Jesus's **example of victory** over satan. "For in that He Himself ... being tempted, He is able to aid those who are tempted" (Hebrews 2:18).

7. Yield the **control** of all your money to God. Give God 10 percent and use the rest with prayer and wisdom. "But those who desire to be rich fall into temptation and a snare, and into many foolish and harmful lusts which drown men in destruction and perdition" (1 Timothy 6:9).

8. Put on the **whole armor** of God. "Put on the whole armor of God, that you may be able to stand against the wiles of the devil" (Ephesians 6:11).

9. Memorize and meditate on **Scripture**. "I have hidden Your word in my heart that I might not sin against You" (Psalm 119:11, NLT).

10. Always **plan** to do right. "Do not be overcome by evil but overcome evil with good" (Romans 12:21).

Lesson 3:

QUESTIONS

PROTECTION AGAINST TEMPTATION

You will not be tempted to sin with any greater enticement than any other believers have faced, but you can be victorious over your temptation. Remember, God is faithful and will not let you be tempted beyond your ability to resist it. He will always make a way to endure it without yielding to it.

1 Corinthians 10:13, ELT

A. THINGS KNOWN ABOUT TEMPTATION

1. _____ . "Let no one say when he is tempted, 'I am tempted by God'; for God cannot be tempted by evil, nor does He Himself tempt anyone" (James 1:13).

2. From _____ . "Your adversary the devil walks about like a roaring lion, seeking whom he may devour" (1 Peter 5:8).

3. Through your _____ . "But each one is tempted when he is drawn away by his own desires and enticed" (James 1:14).

4. Designed to _____ . "Temptation ... when desires have conceived it gives birth to sin, and when sin is full-grown, brings death" (James 1:14-15).

5. Temptation can successfully get to someone _____ . "The devil had already put into the heart of Judas Iscariot ... to betray Him" (John 13:2).

B. WHERE WILL SATAN ATTACK?

Do not love the world or the things in the world. If anyone loves the world, the love of the Father is not in him. For all that is in the world—the lust of the flesh, the lust of the eyes, and the pride of life—is not of the Father but is of the world. (1 John 2:15-16)

1. Lust of the flesh— _____ :

   a. Lust involving things that will _____ the physical body.

   b. This does not include _____ , i.e., food, drink, etc.

2. Lust of the eyes, _____ , attractions, money, possessions, clothes, luxuries, hobbies, etc.

3. Pride of life:

   a. Ego _____ , fame, position, etc.

   b. This does not mean ego, strength, confidence, i.e., to know yourself, your strength, your purpose in life, or your positive contribution.

C. WHAT TO DO IF YOU GIVE IN TO TEMPTATION

1. Your goal is to not sin but be as perfect as possible. "These things I write to you, so that you may not sin" (1 John 2:1).

2. Jesus was perfect; you _____ . Jesus did not give in; _____ .

   a. No one has a perfect _____ . "If we say we have not sinned, we deceive ourselves" (1 John 1:8).

   b. Everyone has been _____ . "Each one is tempted" (James 1:14).

3. Whenever you sin, remember that you have a Savior who _____ . "You have a High Priest who can sympathize with your weakness, He was tempted in all points, but did not sin ... come boldly to His throne to obtain mercy and find grace" (Hebrews 4:15-16, ELT).

4. Confess your sins. "If we confess our sins, He is faithful and just to forgive ... and cleanse" (1 John 1:9).

5. Repent and determine not to _____ . "Create in me a clean heart, O God, and renew a steadfast spirit within me" (Psalm 51:10).

6. God remembers them _____ (see Isaiah 43:35; Jeremiah 31:36; Hebrews 9:12; 10:16-17).

D. TEN THINGS GOD PROVIDES TO RESIST TEMPTATIONS

1. _____ with prayer. "Lead me not into temptation but deliver me from the evil one" (Matthew 6:11, ELT).

2. Begin by _____ to God. "Submit yourselves therefore to God. Resist the devil, and he will flee from you" (James 4:7).

3. Determine to _____ and be firm. "Be sober, be vigilant; because your adversary the devil walks about like a roaring lion, seeking whom he may devour" (1 Peter 5:8).

4. _____ God for victory. "The Lord knows how to rescue the godly" (2 Peter 2:9).

5. Claim Jesus's _____ for you. "For we ... have a High Priest ... let us therefore come boldly to the throne of grace, that we may obtain mercy and find grace to help in time of need" (Hebrews 4:15-16).

6. Follow Jesus's _____ over satan. "For in that He Himself ... being tempted, He is able to aid those who are tempted" (Hebrews 2:18).

7. Yield the _____ of all your money to God. Give God 10 percent and use the rest with prayer and wisdom. "But those who desire to be rich fall into temptation and a snare, and into many foolish and harmful lusts which drown men in destruction and perdition" (1 Timothy 6:9).

8. Put on the _____ of God. "Put on the whole armor of God, that you may be able to stand against the wiles of the devil" (Ephesians 6:11).

9. Memorize and meditate on _____. "I have hidden Your word in my heart that I might not sin against You" (Psalm 119:11, NLT).

10. Always _____ to do right. "Do not be overcome by evil but overcome evil with good" (Romans 12:21).

AFTER OVERCOMING TEMPTATION— VICTORY-LIVING

*But thank God! He ... continues to lead us
along in Christ's triumphal procession.*

2 Corinthians 2:14, NLT

*But thank God! He gives us victory over sin
and death through our Lord Jesus Christ.*

1 Corinthians 15:57, NLT

A. INTRODUCTION

1. Overcoming temptation is **praiseworthy.**

2. Victory-living is better.

3. Victory-living takes **two** **steps**: first, **overcoming** sin; second, **positive** Christian living.

B. LEARNING WHAT NOT TO DO

1. You must not disobey God's commands.

    a. First definition of sin. Sin is my want of **conformity**—into God's law.

    b. Second definition of sin. Sin is **intentionally** breaking God's law.

    c. Types of **disobedience**:

        i. Didn't wash car

        ii. Threw mud on the car

    d. A wise God gives commands for two reasons:

        i. For our **growth**

        ii. For our **protection**

2. You must not violate your conscience.

    a. Why not let your conscience be your guide? "Having their conscience seared [scarred] with a hot iron" (1 Timothy 4:2).

        i. Your conscience may not tell you what is **right**.

        ii. Won't tell you everything that is **wrong**.

        iii. Conscience depends on **training**.

    b. Therefore, to him that knows to do good and does not, it is sin" (James 4:17).

3. You must not harbor impure thoughts.

a. The act of sin usually **begins** in the thought (mind). "Whosoever looketh on a woman to lust ... hath committed adultery in his heart" (Matthew 5:28).

b. Your mind should be **clean**. "Your pure ... devotion to Christ ... corrupted" (2 Corinthians 11:3).

4. You must not **defile** your body.

a. "Give your bodies to God ... a holy living sacrifice ... the kind He will find acceptable" (Romans 12:1, NLT).

b. Don't be childish, "I can do what I want." Don't play in dangerous traffic or in a field with snakes.

5. You must not **link** with those who will make you stumble.

a. "Don't team up with those who are unbelievers ... how can light live with darkness? ... How can a believer be a partner with an unbeliever?" (2 Corinthians 6:14-15, NLT).

b. Be friends with the unsaved, work with them, but don't "link" so that their decisions make you sin or **disobey God**.

6. You must not **negatively** influence others.

a. **Stumbling block**, to cause another to fall. "Take heed ... this liberty of yours becomes a stumbling block to them that are weak" (1 Corinthians 2:9).

b. Early church issue of eating meat offered to idols. "If meat makes my brother offend, I will eat no flesh" (1 Corinthians 8:13).

7. You must be careful of the little things. Illustration: **trash in fuel line**.

C. LEARNING VICTORY-LIVING

1. Let the indwelling Christ give you victory.

    a. "Christ lives in me" (Galatians 2:20). His power gives me (1) **life**, (2) **resistance**.

    b. "I live in this earthly body by trusting in the Son of God who loved me and gave Himself for me" (Galatians 2:20, NLT).

    c. Illustration: child in flaming building. Fireman, "Jump ... I will catch you."

2. Let your new position in Christ give you strength.

    a. "In Christ" 216 times in Paul's letters and 26 times in John. Means: (1) non-experiential position in **Christ's body**, (2) in His **forgiveness**, (3) in His **justification**.

    b. Baptized unto His death, burial, resurrection (see Romans 6:3-11, NLT).

3. Let your new nature control your life.

    a. "If any man be in Christ, he is a new creation" (2 Corinthians 5:17).

    b. You have a new ability to live for Jesus.

    c. Illustration: No **cursing** ... speaking for **Jesus**.

4. Show **gratitude** for what God has done for you. "And whatever you do or say, do it as a representative of the Lord Jesus, giving thanks through him to God the Father" (Colossians 3:17, NLT).

5. Right living maintains a strong Christian testimony. "Abstain from every form of evil" (1 Thessalonians 5:22).

Lesson 4:

QUESTIONS

AFTER OVERCOMING TEMPTATION— VICTORY-LIVING

But thank God! He ... continues to lead us along in Christ's triumphal procession.

2 Corinthians 2:14, NLT

But thank God! He gives us victory over sin and death through our Lord Jesus Christ.

1 Corinthians 15:57, NLT

A. INTRODUCTION

1. Overcoming temptation is _____ .

2. Victory-living is better.

3. Victory-living takes _____ : first, _____ sin; second, _____ Christian living.

B. LEARNING WHAT NOT TO DO

1. You must not disobey God's commands.

    a. First definition of sin. Sin is my want of _____
        —into God's law.

    b. Second definition of sin. Sin is _____ breaking
        God's law.

    c. Types of _____ :

        iv. Didn't wash car

        v. Threw mud on the car

    d. A wise God gives commands for two reasons:

        i. For our _____

        ii. For our _____

2. You must not violate your conscience.

    a. Why not let your conscience be your guide? "Having their
        conscience seared [scarred] with a hot iron" (1 Timothy 4:2).

        i. Your conscience may not tell you what is _____ .

        ii. Won't tell you everything that is _____ .

        iii. Conscience depends on _____ .

    b. Therefore, to him that knows to do good and does not, it is
        sin" (James 4:17).

---

3. You must not harbor impure thoughts.

   a. The act of sin usually _____ in the thought (mind). "Whosoever looketh on a woman to lust ... hath committed adultery in his heart" (Matthew 5:28).

   b. Your mind should be _____ . "Your pure ... devotion to Christ ... corrupted" (2 Corinthians 11:3).

4. You must not _____ your body.

   a. "Give your bodies to God ... a holy living sacrifice ... the kind He will find acceptable" (Romans 12:1, NLT).

   b. Don't be childish, "I can do what I want." Don't play in dangerous traffic or in a field with snakes.

5. You must not _____ with those who will make you stumble.

   a. "Don't team up with those who are unbelievers ... how can light live with darkness? ... How can a believer be a partner with an unbeliever?" (2 Corinthians 6:14-15, NLT).

   b. Be friends with the unsaved, work with them, but don't "link" so that their decisions make you sin or _____ .

6. You must not _____ influence others.

   a. _____ , to cause another to fall. "Take heed ... this liberty of yours becomes a stumbling block to them that are weak" (1 Corinthians 2:9).

   b. Early church issue of eating meat offered to idols. "If meat makes my brother offend, I will eat no flesh" (1 Corinthians 8:13).

7. You must be careful of the little things. Illustration:

_____ .

C. LEARNING VICTORY-LIVING

1. Let the indwelling Christ give you victory.

   a. "Christ lives in me" (Galatians 2:20). His power gives me
      (1) _____ , (2) _____ .

   b. "I live in this earthly body by trusting in the Son of God who
      loved me and gave Himself for me" (Galatians 2:20, NLT).

   c. Illustration: child in flaming building. Fireman, "Jump ... I will
      catch you."

2. Let your new position in Christ give you strength.

   a. "In Christ" 216 times in Paul's letters and 26 times in John.
      Means: (1) non-experiential position in
      _____ , (2) in His _____ ,
      (3) in His _____ .

   b. Baptized unto His death, burial, resurrection (see Romans 6:3-
      11, NLT).

3. Let your new nature control your life.

   a. "If any man be in Christ, he is a new creation" (2 Corinthians
      5:17).

   b. You have a new ability to live for Jesus.

   c. Illustration: No _____ ... speaking for
      _____ .

4. Show _____ for what God has done for you. "And whatever you do or say, do it as a representative of the Lord Jesus, giving thanks through him to God the Father" (Colossians 3:17, NLT).

5. Right living maintains a strong Christian testimony. "Abstain from every form of evil" (1 Thessalonians 5:22).

PART FOUR

TEMPTATION OVERCOMERS

POWERPOINT GUIDE

Slide 1 of 49

Temptation Overcomers

By: Elmer Towns

Slide 2 of 49

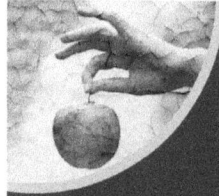

Lesson 1

The Consequences of Giving Into Temptation

Slide 3 of 49

"Now the serpent was more cunning than any beast of the field which the Lord God had made. And he said to the woman, 'Has God indeed said, You shall not eat of every tree of the garden?' And the woman said to the serpent, 'We may eat the fruit of the trees of the garden; but of the fruit of the tree, which is in the midst of the garden, God has said, You shall not eat it, nor shall you touch it, lest you die.' Then the serpent said to the woman, 'You will not surely die. For God knows that in the day you eat of it your eyes will be opened, and you will be like God, knowing good and evil'"
Genesis 3:1-5, NKJV

Slide 4 of 49

A. WHAT IS TEMPTATION?

1. Webster's definition: "To seduce, entice, or persuade."
   a. The source will hide its intent.
   b. The object of temptation – the naïve.
   c. Original meaning – to attract with gratification (i.e., what you are). To do that which is not intended or not natural.

Slide 5 of 49

2. The serpent/satan wanted Eve to do what he originally did deny/disobey God.

3. Why target the woman? "Said to the woman" (v. 1). Stronger emotions/feelings/sensitivity.

4. Original approach – "Has God said?" (v. 1). Created doubt.

Slide 6 of 49

5. Webster's meaning of doubt. "To be uncertain, hesitant, questionable. Original "to fear or to scare."

6. Temptation's threefold strategy:
   a. Added to God's Word. "Touch it" (v. 3).
   b. Altered. "You shall surely die" (2:17). "Lest you die" (3:3).
   c. Omitted. "In the day" (2:17).

Slide 7 of 49

7. God told Adam (Genesis 2:15-17):
   a. Did Adam not communicate clearly to Eve?
   b. Did Eve not hear and understand?

8. Half-truth: "You will not surely die" (vv. 3-4). Die spiritually not physical.

9. Temptation's results:
   a. New awareness/attractions, "eyes opened" (v. 5).
   b. To understand as proven, "knowing good and evil" (v. 5).

Slide 8 of 49

B. THREE-FOLD TEMPTATION

1. Lust/desire of flesh, i.e., physical, "good for food." Needed to continue physical life.

2. Lust/desire of eyes, i.e., emotional, good for happiness, needed internal satisfaction.

3. Lust/desire of pride, good to protect or enhance self-awareness.

1. Awareness of both -- knew their spiritual positive, and physical negative passions.

2. Awareness to "hide" their new physical passion. "They knew they were naked" (3:7). They made clothes.

3. God consciousness. "They heard the sound of the LORD God walking ... presence of the LORD God" (3:8).

Slide 9 of 49

4. "God called" (3:9). God knew:
   a. What they did.
   b. Where they were hiding.
   c. What He was going to do.
   d. And to fix responsibly, "who told you that you were naked?" (v. 7).

Slide 10 of 49

5. Pass the buck:
   a. Adam, "The woman You gave me ... I ate" (v. 12).
   b. Eve, "the serpent deceived me" (v. 13).

Slide 11 of 49

6. The serpent:
   a. "On your belly" (v. 19)
   b. Conflict. "And I will put enmity between you and the woman, And between your seed and her Seed; He shall bruise your head, and you shall bruise His heel" (3:15).
   c. Her seed, proto evangelium (Latin), first giving of the gospel.

Slide 12 of 49

7. Eve:
   a. Pain. "Sorrows ...bring forth children" (v. 16).
   b. Submissive. "You desire ... husband" (3:16).

8. Adam, hard work, "thorns ... sweat ..." (vv. 18-19).

Slide 13 of 49

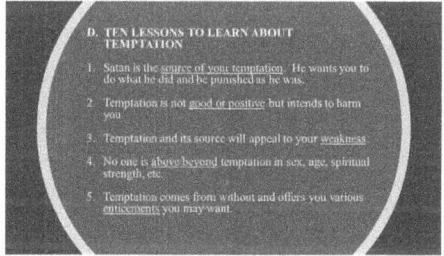

D. TEN LESSONS TO LEARN ABOUT TEMPTATION

1. Satan is the source of your temptation. He wants you to do what he did and be punished as he was.

2. Temptation is not good or positive but intends to harm you.

3. Temptation and its source will appeal to your weakness.

4. No one is above/beyond temptation in sex, age, spiritual strength, etc.

5. Temptation comes from without and offers you various enticements you may want.

Slide 14 of 49

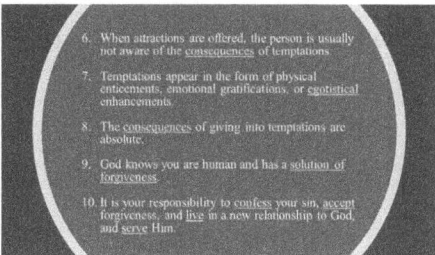

6. When attractions are offered, the person is usually not aware of the consequences of temptations.

7. Temptations appear in the form of physical enticements, emotional gratifications, or egotistical enhancements.

8. The consequences of giving into temptations are absolute.

9. God knows you are human and has a solution of forgiveness.

10. It is your responsibility to confess your sin, accept forgiveness, and live in a new relationship to God, and serve Him.

Slide 15 of 49

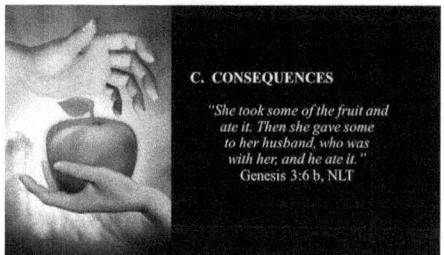

C. CONSEQUENCES

"She took some of the fruit and ate it. Then she gave some to her husband, who was with her, and he ate it." Genesis 3:6 b, NLT

Slide 16 of 49

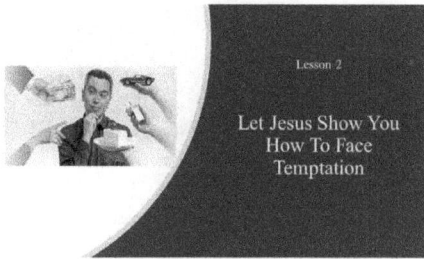

Lesson 2

Let Jesus Show You
How To Face
Temptation

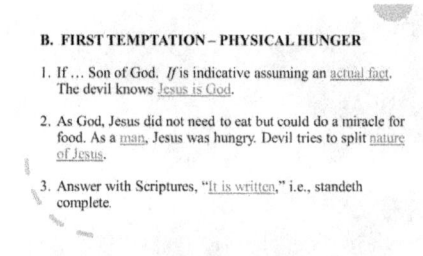

"Jesus was led by the Spirit into the wilderness to be tempted by the devil ... fasted forty days and forty nights, afterwards ... hungry. The tempter said 'if You are the Son of God ... stones become bread. Jesus ... 'It is written man shall not live by bread alone, but by every word ... mouth of God.' Devil took Him to holy city ... 'if You are the Son of God ... throw Yourself down, for it is written He shall give His angels charge over You ... they shall bear You up lest You dash Your foot against a stone.' Jesus ... 'it is written, you shall not tempt the LORD your God.' Again, devil... exceedingly high mountain ...'all this I will give You, if You will fall down and worship me.' Jesus ... 'it is written, you shall worship the LORD your God and Him only' ... devil left him."
Matthew 4:1-11, NKJV

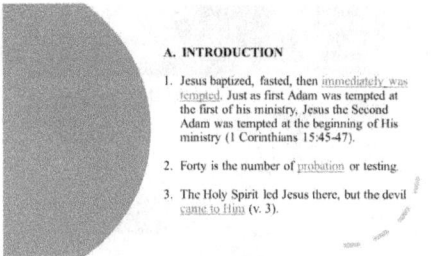

A. INTRODUCTION

1. Jesus baptized, fasted, then immediately was tempted. Just as first Adam was tempted at the first of his ministry, Jesus the Second Adam was tempted at the beginning of His ministry (1 Corinthians 15:45-47).

2. Forty is the number of probation or testing.

3. The Holy Spirit led Jesus there, but the devil came to Him (v. 3).

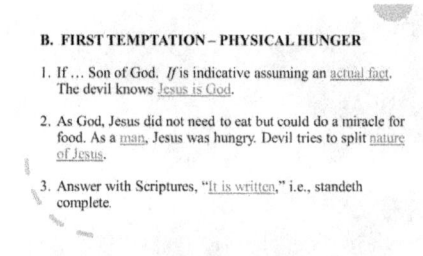

B. FIRST TEMPTATION – PHYSICAL HUNGER

1. If ... Son of God. *If* is indicative assuming an actual fact. The devil knows Jesus is God.

2. As God, Jesus did not need to eat but could do a miracle for food. As a man, Jesus was hungry. Devil tries to split nature of Jesus.

3. Answer with Scriptures, "It is written," i.e., standeth complete.

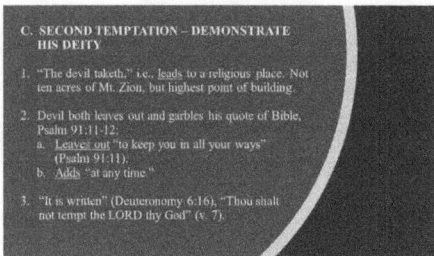

C. SECOND TEMPTATION – DEMONSTRATE HIS DEITY

1. "The devil taketh," i.e., leads to a religious place. Not ten acres of Mt. Zion, but highest point of building.

2. Devil both leaves out and garbles his quote of Bible, Psalm 91:11-12:
   a. Leaves out "to keep you in all your ways" (Psalm 91:11).
   b. Adds "at any time."

3. "It is written" (Deuteronomy 6:16), "Thou shalt not tempt the LORD thy God" (v. 7).

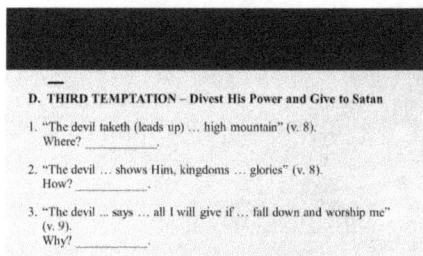

D. THIRD TEMPTATION – Divest His Power and Give to Satan

1. "The devil taketh (leads up) ... high mountain" (v. 8). Where? _____.

2. "The devil ... shows Him, kingdoms ... glories" (v. 8). How? _____.

3. "The devil ... says ... all I will give if ... fall down and worship me" (v. 9). Why? _____.

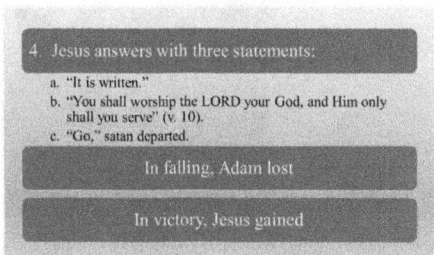

4. Jesus answers with three statements:

a. "It is written."
b. "You shall worship the LORD your God, and Him only shall you serve" (v. 10).
c. "Go," satan departed.

In falling, Adam lost

In victory, Jesus gained

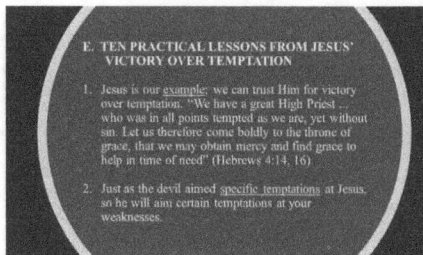

E. TEN PRACTICAL LESSONS FROM JESUS' VICTORY OVER TEMPTATION

1. Jesus is our example; we can trust Him for victory over temptation. "We have a great High Priest ... who was in all points tempted as we are, yet without sin. Let us therefore come boldly to the throne of grace, that we may obtain mercy and find grace to help in time of need" (Hebrews 4:14, 16).

2. Just as the devil aimed specific temptations at Jesus, so he will aim certain temptations at your weaknesses.

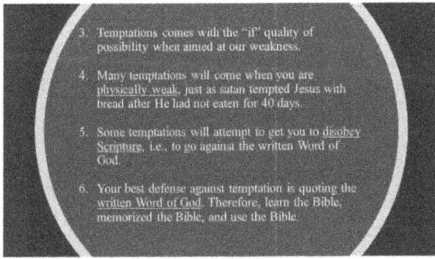

3. Temptations comes with the "if" quality of possibility when aimed at our weakness.

4. Many temptations will come when you are physically weak, just as satan tempted Jesus with bread after He had not eaten for 40 days.

5. Some temptations will attempt to get you to disobey Scripture, i.e., to go against the written Word of God.

6. Your best defense against temptation is quoting the written Word of God. Therefore, learn the Bible, memorized the Bible, and use the Bible.

Slide 25 of 49

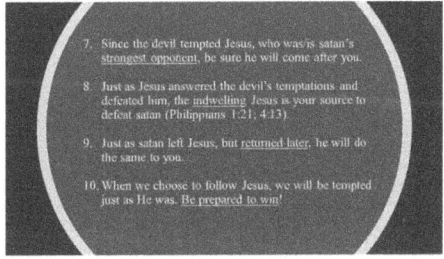

7. Since the devil tempted Jesus, who was/is satan's strongest opponent, be sure he will come after you.

8. Just as Jesus answered the devil's temptations and defeated him, the indwelling Jesus is your source to defeat satan (Philippians 1:21; 4:13).

9. Just as satan left Jesus, but returned later, he will do the same to you.

10. When we choose to follow Jesus, we will be tempted just as He was. Be prepared to win!

Slide 26 of 49

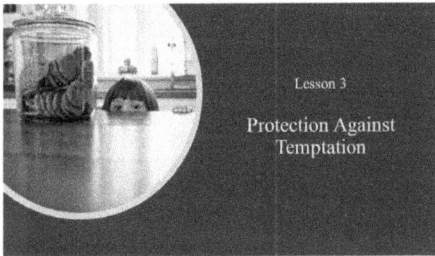

Lesson 3

Protection Against Temptation

Slide 27 of 49

"You will not be tempted to sin with any greater enticement than any other believers have faced, but you can be victorious over your temptation. Remember God is faithful and will not let you be tempted beyond your ability to resist it. He will always make a way to endure it without yielding to it"
1 Corinthians 10:13, ELT

Slide 28 of 49

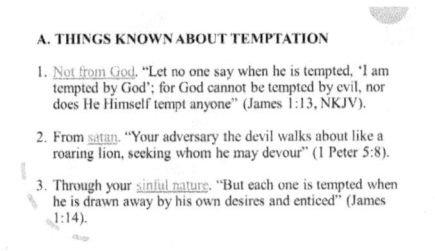

A. THINGS KNOWN ABOUT TEMPTATION

1. Not from God. "Let no one say when he is tempted, 'I am tempted by God'; for God cannot be tempted by evil, nor does He Himself tempt anyone" (James 1:13, NKJV).

2. From satan. "Your adversary the devil walks about like a roaring lion, seeking whom he may devour" (1 Peter 5:8).

3. Through your sinful nature. "But each one is tempted when he is drawn away by his own desires and enticed" (James 1:14).

Slide 29 of 49

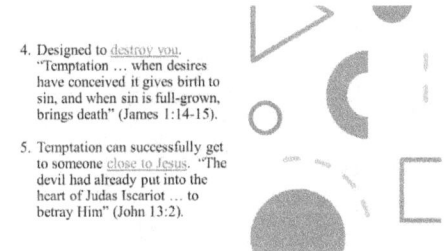

4. Designed to destroy you. "Temptation ... when desires have conceived it gives birth to sin, and when sin is full-grown, brings death" (James 1:14-15).

5. Temptation can successfully get to someone close to Jesus. "The devil had already put into the heart of Judas Iscariot ... to betray Him" (John 13:2).

Slide 30 of 49

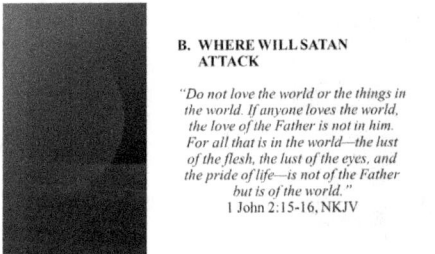

B. WHERE WILL SATAN ATTACK

"Do not love the world or the things in the world. If anyone loves the world, the love of the Father is not in him. For all that is in the world—the lust of the flesh, the lust of the eyes, and the pride of life—is not of the Father but is of the world."
1 John 2:15-16, NKJV

Slide 31 of 49

1. Lust of the flesh – physical:
   a. Lust involving things that will please the physical body.
   b. This does not include necessities, i.e., food, drink, etc.

2. Lust of the eyes, things, attractions, money, possessions, clothes, luxuries, hobbies, etc.

3. Pride of life:
   a. Ego enhancement, fame, position, etc.
   b. This does not mean ego strength confidence, i.e., to know yourself, your strength, your purpose in life or your positive contribution.

Slide 32 of 49

C. WHAT TO DO IF YOU GIVE INTO TEMPTATION

1. Your goal is to not sin but be as perfect as possible. "These things I write to you, so that you may not sin" (1 John 2:1).

2. Jesus was perfect, you are not, Jesus did not give in, you might.
   a. No one has a perfect "track record." "If we say we have not sinned, we deceive ourselves" (1 John 1:8).
   b. Everyone has been tempted. "Each one is tempted" (James 1:14).

Slide 33 of 49

3. Whenever you sin, remember you have a Savior who understands. "You have a High Priest who can sympathize with your weakness, He was tempted in all points, but did not sin ... come boldly to His throne to obtain mercy and find grace" (Hebrews 4:15-16, ELT).

4. Confess your sins. "If we confess our sins, He is faithful and just to forgive ... and cleanse" (1 John 1:9).

Slide 34 of 49

5. Repent and determine not to do it again. "Create in me a clean heart, O God, and renew a steadfast spirit within me" (Psalm 51:10, NKJV).

6. God remembers them no more. (Isaiah 43:35; Jeremiah 31:36; Hebrews 9:12, 10:16-17).

Slide 35 of 49

D. TEN THINGS GOD PROVIDES TO RESIST TEMPTATIONS

1. Prepare with prayer. "Lead me not into temptation but deliver me from the evil one" (Matthew 6:13, ELT).

2. Begin by yielding to God. "Submit yourselves therefore to God. Resist the devil, and he will flee from you" (James 4:7).

3. Determine to resist and be firm. "Be sober, be vigilant; because your adversary the devil walks about like a roaring lion, seeking whom he may devour" (1 Peter 5:8, NKJV).

4. Trust God for victory. "The Lord knows how to rescue the godly" (2 Peter 2:9).

Slide 36 of 49

5. Claim Jesus intercession for you. "For we ... have a High Priest ... let us therefore come boldly to the throne of grace, that we may obtain mercy and find grace to help in time of need" (Hebrews 4:15-16).

6. Follow Jesus' example of victory over satan. "For in that He Himself ... being tempted, He is able to aid those who are tempted" (Hebrews 2:18).

7. Yield the control of all your money to God. Give God 10% and use the rest with prayer and wisdom. "But those who desire to be rich fall into temptation and a snare, and into many foolish and harmful lusts which drown men in destruction and perdition" (1 Timothy 6:9).

Slide 37 of 49

8. Put on the whole armor of God. "Put on the whole armor of God, that you may be able to stand against the wiles of the devil" (Ephesians 6:11).

9. Memorize and mediate on Scripture. "I have hidden Your word in my heart that I might not sin against You" (Psalm 119:11, NLT).

10. Always plan to do right. "Do not be overcome by evil but overcome evil with good" (Romans 12:21).

Slide 38 of 49

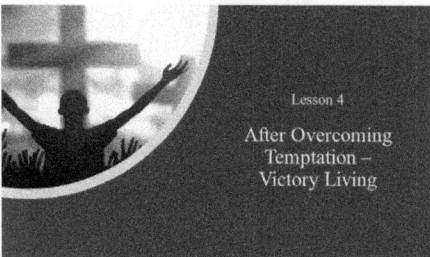

Lesson 4

After Overcoming Temptation – Victory Living

Slide 39 of 49

"But thank God! He ... continues to lead us along in Christ's triumphal procession."
2 Corinthians 2:14, NLT

"But thank God! He gives us victory over sin and death through our Lord Jesus Christ."
1 Corinthians 15:57, NLT

Slide 40 of 49

Slide 41 of 49

A. INTRODUCTION

1. Overcoming temptation is praiseworthy.

2. Victory-living is better.

3. Victory-living takes two-steps. First, overcoming sin; second positive Christian living.

Slide 42 of 49

B. LEARNING WHAT NOT TO DO

1. You must not disobey God's commands.
   a. First definition of sin. Sin is my want of conformity – into God's law.
   b. Second definition of sin. Sin is intentionally breaking God's law.
   c. Types of disobedience:
      (1) Didn't wash care
      (2) Threw mud on the car
   d. A wise God gives commands for two reasons:
      (1) For our growth
      (2) For our protection

Slide 43 of 49

2. You must not violate your conscience.
   a. Why not let your conscience be your guide? "Having their conscience seared (scared) with a hot iron" (1 Timothy 4:2).
      (1) Your conscience may not tell you what is right.
      (2) Won't tell you everything that is wrong.
      (3) Conscience depends on training.
   b. Therefore, to him that knowns to do good and does not, it is sin" (James 4:17).

Slide 44 of 49

3. You must not harbor impure thoughts.
   a. The act of sin usually begins in the thought (mind). "Whosoever, looketh on a woman to lust ... hath committed adultery in his heart" (Matthew 5:28).
   b. Your mind should be clean. "Your pure ... devotion to Christ ... corrupted" (2 Corinthians 11:3).

4. You must not defile your body.
   a. "Give your bodies to God ... a holy living sacrifice ... the kind He will find acceptable" (Romans 12:1, NLT).
   b. Don't be childish, "I can do what I want." Don't play in dangerous traffic or in a field with snakes.

Slide 45 of 49

5. You must not link with those who will make you stumble.
   a. "Don't team up with those who are unbelievers ... how can light live with darkness? ... How can a believer be a partner with an unbeliever?" (2 Corinthians 6:14-15, NLT).
   b. Be friends with the unsaved, work with them but don't "link" so their decisions make you sin or disobey God.

Slide 46 of 49

6. You must not negatively influence others.
   a. Stumbling block, to cause another to fall. "Take heed ... this liberty of yours becomes a stumbling block to them that are weak" (1 Corinthians 2:9).
   b. Early church issue of eating meat offered to idols. "If meat makes my brother offend, I will eat no flesh" (1 Corinthians 8:13).

7. You must be careful to little things. Illustration: trash in fuel line.

Slide 47 of 49

C. LEARNING VICTORY-LIVING

1. Let the indwelling Christ give you victory.
   a. "Christ lives in me" (Galatians 2:20). His power gives me, (1) life, (2) resistance.
   b. "I live in this earthly body by trusting in the Son of God who loved me and gave Himself for me" (Galatians 2:20, NLT).
   c. Illustration: child in flaming building. Fireman, "Jump ... I will catch you."

Slide 48 of 49

2. Let your new position in Christ give you strength.
   a. "In Christ" 216 times in Paul's letters, and 26 times in John. Means: (1) non-experiential position in Christ's body, (2) in His forgiveness, (3) in His justification.
   b. Baptized unto His death, burial, resurrection (Romans 6:3-11, NLT).

3. Let your new nature control your life.
   a. "If any man be in Christ, he is a new creation" (2 Corinthians 5:17).
   b. You have a new ability to live for Jesus.
   c. Illustration: No cursing ... speaking for Jesus.

4. Show gratitude for what God has done for you. "And whatever you do or say, do it as a representative of the Lord Jesus, giving thanks through him to God the Father." (Colossians 3:17, NLT).

5. Right living maintains a strong Christian testimony. "Abstain from every form of evil" (1 Thessalonians 5:22).

Slide 49 of 49

PART FIVE

TEMPTATION OVERCOMERS

ADDITIONAL RESOURCES

POWERPOINT SLIDES:

To purchase and download the Powerpoint Slides go to
https://www.norimediagroup.com/pages/elmer-towns

VIDEO:

To purchase available video by Dr. Towns go to
https://www.norimediagroup.com/pages/elmer-towns

ADD-ON CONTENT

To purchase additional products in this series go to
https://www.norimediagroup.com/pages/elmer-towns

RELATED BOOKS

My Name is the Holy Spirit: Discover Me through My Name
Available at https://www.norimediagroup.com/pages/elmer-towns

From

ELMER L. TOWNS

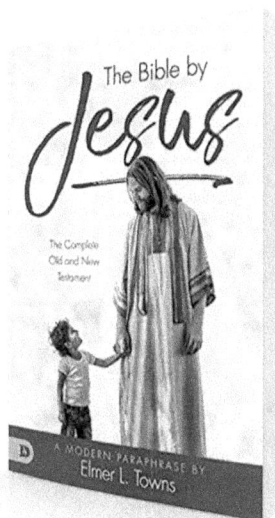

The Bible is the only answer that can satisfy the longing of every human heart

The Bible by Jesus is a unique presentation of the Scriptures from the perspective of Jesus the Author Himself. This powerful paraphrase of the Old and New Testaments will usher you into a fresh level of intimate experience with God through His Word.

You will see Christ in every book of the Bible. Then you will understand Scripture that transforms your life.

- Encounter the Old Testament as a gateway to know Jesus.
- Read to hear the voice of Jesus speaking through the Gospel as He tells you of His birth, ministry, death and resurrection.
- Experience Acts, the epistles, and the book of Revelation to know Jesus and His will for our life.

Read the pages of Scripture to hear the Son of God Himself and draw near to encounter His presence.

Purchase your copy wherever books are sold

From

ELMER L. TOWNS

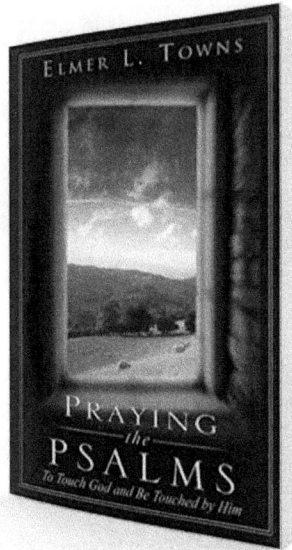

The Book of Psalms reflects the heart of God. *Praying the Psalms* carefully shapes the Psalms into personal prayers enabling you to identify with the Psalmist as he prayed. The author, Dr. Towns, is living breathing testimony of the power and fulfillment you will experience as you read the pages of this most powerful book.

The Psalmist poured our his soul to God concerning the things that deeply moved him. As you read the Psalms, you are taking a peak into his heart. You will weep when he weeps, should when he rejoices, burn when he gets angry and fall on your face when he worships God.

Purchase your copy wherever books are sold

www.ingramcontent.com/pod-product-compliance
Lightning Source LLC
Chambersburg PA
CBHW072007090426
42740CB00011B/2125